MBI Publishing Company

MUSCLE CAR COLOR HISTORY

SHELBY MUSTANG

Tom Corcoran

MBI Publishing Company books are also available at discounts in bulk quantity for industrial or sales-promotional use. For details write to Special Sales Manager at Motorbooks International Wholesalers & Distributors, 729 Prospect Avenue, PO Box 1, Osceola, WI 54020-0001 USA

Library of Congress Cataloging-in-Publication Data

Corcoran, Tom.
    Shelby mustang / Tom Corcoran.
    p.   cm.—(MBI Publishing Company muscle car color history)
    ISBN 0-87938-620-7
    1. Mustang automobile—History.
2. Shelby automobile—History.
I. Title   II. Series.
TL215.M8C68   1992
629.222'2—dc20   92-19302

On the front cover: The first edition, 1965 Shelby Mustang GT-350 in the classic Wimbledon White with Guardsman Blue Le Mans racing stripes. *Tom Corcoran*

On the frontispiece: Competition Shelby Mustang 5R104, owned by Jim Bridges.

On the title page: A 1968 Shelby Cobra GT-500 convertible.

On the back cover: Three classic Shelby Mustangs: a 1965 GT-350 R-Model; 1966 GT-350H Hertz Rent-a-Racer; and a 1970 GT-350, the last of the line.

Printed in Singapore through PH Productions Pte. Ltd.

Contents

Hertz Rent A Car promotional photograph from 1968 to announce the arrival of the new Shelby GT 350 model available for rental.

Acknowledgments

No book of this nature is created by one person. Because I have long been intrigued by the uniqueness of Mustangs, this study of the 1965-1970 Shelby began for me as a photographic exercise. I enjoyed the details, and Donald Farr of Dobbs Publications, then editor of *Mustang Monthly*, gave me my first encouragement to keep at it. Putting words on paper came with the deal, so Donald is again to thank for keeping me primed (of course I must accept all blame for the quality of the text). To Larry Dobbs, who gave me the only real job I've ever had (my mother always dreamed I'd work in an office), I offer gratitude for his confidence and willingness to approach the world of Mustangs and Shelbys in exciting ways.

I would like to point out several people who have offered support beyond the call of duty: Dan Gerber, a fountain of information from his days as both an independent racer and a Shelby team member; the late Lee Cigler of Billings, Montana, whose infectious enthusiasm touched all Mustang and Shelby fans; Earl Davis, whose technical wizardry and tutoring over the years has proved invaluable; Don and Tot Buck from New Orleans, folks with a constantly positive outlook, who love to see the Shelbys at speed; Rob Reaser, my associate at *Mustang Monthly*, whose dependable efforts allowed me the mental space for this book; Bruce Weiss of Melbourne, Florida, a closet perfectionist with a constantly helping hand; Rick Kopec, co-director of the Shelby American Automobile Club (SAAC), for his carefully researched *Shelby American World Registry* (c/o SAAC, PO Box 681, Sharon, CT 06069) as well as his ongoing efforts to keep the world of Shelby alive and kicking; Paul Zazarine at Dobbs Publications for aiming me into this project; Bob Perkins of Juneau, Wisconsin, for his unending contribution of knowledge to the hobby and for steering my camera toward many fine automobiles; and Michael Dregni at Motorbooks International, for his patience and wisdom.

Over the past ten years, many car owners, club members, automotive journalists, restorers, and parts vendors have helped to shape my ideas regarding the evolution of the Shelby Mustangs and the state of today's Shelby scene. The cars are the core of both a significant international hobby and a thriving mini-world of business. I owe a debt of gratitude to everyone I've met in my years on the trail of Mustangs and Shelbys, especially Drew Alcazar, Bob Aliberto, John Craft, Lauren Jonas Fix, Pete Geisler, Ray Hamilton, Walt Hane, Jerry Heasley, Peter Klutt, Melvin Little, Scott McNair, Paul Newitt, Jan Orme, Richard Porter, Frank Reynolds, and Tom Wilson.

A special thanks must go to the car owners. Without their willing cooperation there would be no photographs, there would be no book. Many thanks to Debbie Ames, Steve Ames, Bill Anziani, Bill Blank, Grant Blohm, Dick Bridges, Jim Bridges, Don Buck, Gary Burke, Gary Childress, Judy Cigler, Lyle Cigler, Mack Darr, Frank Davis, Ken Eber, Cliff Ernst, Bob Estes, Paul Fix, Rich Florence, Shannon Florence, Dan Foiles, Brian Freeman, Gilbert Funk, Carl Gocksch, Mickey Graphia, Bob Hoover, John Jackson, Bob Jennings, Carol Jennings, Wayne Johnson, Colleen Kopec, Rick Kopec, Bruce Larson, Dan Lawless, Tommy Moore, Jim Osborn, Bob Perkins, Corky Reynolds, Frank Reynolds, Perry Rushing, Adam Scheps, Carroll Shelby, Bob Spedale, Jack Staples, Ron Starnes, Bob Steinberg, Bob Thrower, Owen Tomlinson, Tom Van Wagner, Robert Vance, John Brad Wagner, Bruce Weiss, Karen Weiss, Mike Williams, Pete Wolff, and Steve Yates. If I have omitted any deserving person from these rosters, I blame it on the fumes and apologize in advance.

This book is for everyone who has skinned a knuckle working on a Shelby, and has experienced the goose bumps while listening to, watching, riding in, or driving a Shelby Mustang.

—*Tom Corcoran*

Introduction:
Cobra Meets Mustang

The Shelby Is Born

Entrepreneurs feed on dreams of success. They see vacancies in the marketplace, and work to create products to meet those consumer needs. That kind of pioneering requires a blend of risk, knowledge, experience, hope for profit, confidence in methods and, for sanity's sake, a sense of fun. Carroll Shelby, with the Cobra roadsters, had that blend. His successes led to further collaboration with Ford Motor Company, in a project to promote the hot new 1964½ Mustang.

The story of Shelby's entry into automobile manufacturing has been told in hundreds of magazine articles and two

The 1964½ Mustang, with its long hood, short trunk, bucket seats, and floor-mounted shifter, was introduced on April 17, 1964. The eye-catching cars were featured on the covers of Time *and* Newsweek, *and Ford dealers racked up sales records from the first week onward. Hailed as an all-American sports car, the Mustang was available by early summer with the 271hp High Performance 289ci engine. But Ford felt the Mustang's overall image needed a strong boost to carry it into the 1965 sales season. As events developed, the astounding and raucous Shelby GT-350 would provide the victories and the headlines that Ford's marketers wanted.*

dozen books. It is such a modern-day little guy, big guy fable—the gutsy and foresighted individual in partnership with one of the largest corporations in the world—that it has taken on the trappings of legend. The story will be retold well into the future, with embellishments as well as omissions, with new information and diehard fictions. I hope to present it simply and correctly.

In the Beginning,
There Was the Cobra

No automotive history begins on the first day of production. The Mustang was introduced to America on April 17, 1964, and its origins precede that date by several years. The Shelby GT-350s commenced production in the first months of 1965, but their history easily predates that of the standard Mustang. During the mid-to-late-1950s, Shelby enjoyed a remarkable competitive driving career, with three national championships in sports cars, a spot on the Aston Martin team, and significant victories in Europe that included a 1959 win at the 24 Hours of Le Mans. During those years, he established a memorable image: a lanky Texas chicken farmer in overalls and cowboy hat. He would scratch his head, say, "Aw, shucks" (or something spicier), and then go out and win a race.

BUY IT!..... OR WATCH IT GO BY!

Buy It! Or Watch It Go By! Inspired by an enthusiast magazine advertisement, the author sent away for one of the first Shelby AC Cobra brochures. The roadster's $5,995 price tag was stratospheric for a twenty-year-old, but the brochure remained a keeper. Ironically, in Ford's initial promotional efforts for the 1993 Mustang Cobra, with its 5.0liter GT-40 engine package, no mention of Carroll Shelby was made to link the Cobra name to its origins.

After the race, he would "Shucks" some more, but he was no country fool.

Shelby astutely recognized that although they were agile, most European sports cars lacked the raw torque available in small American engines. He knew that combining proper handling with abundant, lightweight power would create a winner. Unfortunately, when he tried to act upon those first ideas (in a proposal said to involve General Motors' eight-cylinder Corvette engine and chassis), his efforts were stymied. Others laughed at his ideas, and he did not have the hard cash to pursue his plan. Still, the concept remained on his mind.

Not long after the Le Mans pinnacle, health problems forced Shelby into retirement. A coronary condition that would lead to numerous bypass operations (and, finally, a 1991 heart transplant at Cedars-Sinai Hospital in Los Angeles), caused the doctors to disqualify him from competition. This setback did nothing to quench his

Carroll Shelby's personal automobile collection includes the first 260ci AC Cobra and this 427 Cobra. This big-block roadster was among the undetermined number of 427 Cobras originally built with 428ci engines.

spirit. He found several business opportunities in California, but still wanted to build that small pocket of horsepower.

In 1960, after learning that Ford had developed a 221ci V-8, he kicked into high gear. He mentally pictured that engine in something like an Austin-Healey, a car weighing 2,500lb or less. After a few months of investigative legwork, some help from friend and future associate Lew Spencer, a few prospective designs, and some shuffling of ideas, Shelby finally put it together. In 1961, he convinced both AC Cars in England and Ford Motor Company in Detroit that he could combine the AC chassis and Ford's small-block engine to create a world-class sports car.

The Cobra was born. Shelby pulled it off with the thinnest of budgets, a great sense of how to deal with the automotive media, and occasional sleights of hand. But he made it work. Not only did his boardroom and telephone tap dances turn executives into believers and reporters into supporters, but Shelby leapt past his goal and took his enterprise years into the future, into realms of production and racing conquest no one imagined at the start. The 260 Cobras (with performance versions of the 260ci Fairlane engine), 289 Cobras, Cobra Daytona Coupes, King Co-

bras, 427 Cobras, and selected Ford GT-40s forged their marks on the automotive world.

One should never imagine that Shelby lost his eye for the long term. His sense of doing business always stressed survival, and the only sure way to ensure longevity is either to make money or to make the money people happy. The "Cobra-Mustang" deal out of which the Shelby Mustang was born is proof of Shelby's success. In the beginning, it was the man who went hat-in-hand to Ford to propose the AC Cobra. Several years later, in 1964, it was Ford who went to the man. The corporation saw Shelby as the individual best suited to spark the Mustang image.

Carroll Shelby delivered enough excitement and adventure in the 1960s to secure elevated status in the history of both American and worldwide automobile manufacturing. He created ideas, cars, and teams. A fighter, a thinker, a winner, and a champion, Shelby did the job. The legend deserves to grow, and will expand with the passing of time.

Shelby and the Mustang

Introduced in April 1964 with floor-mounted shifters and bucket seats, the Ford Mustang appealed to a broad cross section of the public. Stylish and sized for a personal touch, the cars appealed to sporty minded buyers of all ages. They could be delivered as economical six-cylinders with minimal options. Or they could be eight-cylinder automatics with deluxe interiors, perhaps with air conditioning or a center console. For special enthusiasts, Mustangs were available with four-speed transmissions and 271hp High Performance (or "Hi-Po") engines.

One year after that April 1964 debut, Ford introduced the Mustang GT package

with its stiff suspension, dual exhausts, and front disc brakes. The combination of a Hi-Po 289ci V-8, the GT option package, and a four-speed transmission offered a genuine sports package. To purchase such a vehicle, someone had to have both desire for extra performance and additional dollars to pay for the options.

Naturally, with each step up the ladder of Mustang style and power, the cost of a car increased. Fewer buyers stepped forward. The Shelby Mustang, at the top rung of that ladder, effectively converted a snappy boulevard touring car into a gutsy, stiff, loud, and incredibly fast street-legal race car. The price was premium and the product was primitive. So when Carroll Shelby, in the summer of 1965, positioned the first GT-350s, the folks placing orders must have been a rare bunch, indeed.

It is fairly well known that as time passed, Ford Motor Company exerted increasing influence on the makeup, design, and marketing of the Shelby Mustangs. Over that period of approximately five years, Shelby became disenchanted with his project. For him, the concept became diluted and sour. He thought that the cars had become oversized, overproduced, and out of his control. It is a salute to his initial conception that no matter how Shelby perceived the situation and despite Ford's attempts to make the vehicles luxurious and easily marketable, the cars remained distinctive to the end. Of course, the end came in late 1969, by Shelby's request.

Even before then, Ford and Shelby fans knew how special and distinctive the cars were. Many realized that with governmental regulations and insurance industry pressures mounting, Detroit was unlikely ever to produce another factory race car. Some may have hoped that the Shelbys would be "worth something" down the

Mix a Mustang with a Cobra . . . When the December 1964 Hot Rod *hit the newsstands, the Shelby GT-350 project was still in development. Yet, this ad proves Ford's eagerness to blend the Shelby image with the Mustang name. This early offering of Cobra brand speed equipment also promoted the Fastback that had been introduced to the Mustang line in September.*

road. Surely, few suspected that the uniqueness of the factory-built hot rods, the mystique of the Ferrari-beating company from California, and the enduring respect for Carroll Shelby would elevate prices so astoundingly. The Shelby's value at the beginning was founded on power, looks, and ability to win. Their value today is derived from the fact that nothing like them has appeared since.

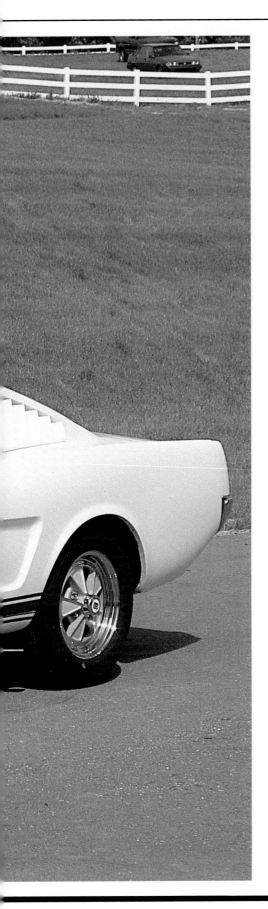

1965 Shelby GT-350

Built for the Track. Sold for the Street

The Shelby GT-350, a high-performance version of the smash hit 1964½ and 1965 Mustangs, was created to help Ford beat the competition in dealer showrooms. The GT-350 racing models whipped opponents everywhere else, too.

Detroit always has valued its charade of industrial espionage, the endless insider talk that fires up market strategy and stokes the flames of product development. In mid-1964, Ford knew it had a winner with the Mustang. Its bucket seats, floor-mounted shifter, long hood, and personal size had won so many admirers that the hardtops and convertibles set sales records from the first introductory hoopla. But planners recognized that sales of a "one-trick pony" could suffer when other manufacturers introduced similar vehicles. They had heard the rumors and seen the "spy" photos. Barracudas were in the stores; the

Created by Shelby American engineers from a 271hp Mustang Fastback, the 1965 Shelby Mustang offered enthusiasts a tough, loud racing vehicle straight from a Ford dealer's showroom. Its modified suspension, engine, and interior were not immediately obvious, but the twin Guardsman Blue Le Mans racing stripes announced the GT-350 as something other than a standard Mustang.

Camaros and Firebirds were on the way. Market position was sure to be threatened, and the Mustang's success, a huge corporate victory, needed to be preserved.

That August, with assembly plants phased out of 1964½ Mustang production and already building the 1965 Mustangs with alternators instead of generators, different engine and color choices, and trim changes, the marketers were faced with a new round of promotion. Checkered flags seemed an exciting theme.

Starting With a Blank Slate

Ford's ongoing projects with Carroll Shelby, the established Cobra 289 production run, the winning race programs involving small-block Cobras, Daytona Coupes, and King Cobras, and the 427 Cobras on the verge of production, made it natural for the company to approach the man who had working knowledge. Ford wanted an upgraded Mustang with power, flash, and, if possible, immediate racing victories. By then, Shelby had seen almost four years of wrestling with production headaches, bending, molding, and adapting to the racing rules of various sanctioning bodies, and making incredibly quick and perceptive decisions. Survival had forced him to master cost effectiveness, public relations,

and plain old going faster in straight lines and corners. He got the call.

The blank slate would be the Mustang Fastback, the "2 + 2" model new to the Mustang lineup with the introduction of the 1965 models. To qualify the GT-350 for SCCA B/Production competition, a process called homologation, Shelby American would have to produce at least 100 cars before the end of 1964.

Beginning in June that year, Ford had offered its High Performance 271hp 289ci engine in the Mustang. Shelby felt that a street version would be needed to sell 100 cars, so, with a powerful engine already covered by Ford factory warranty, Shelby elected to go easy on the powerplant and to concentrate on modifying the Mustang's handling characteristics to accommodate both racing and street situations. Within the safety envelope, street comforts would be secondary to performance. Of course, the cars built specifically for competition would be hard-core and expensive. But the racing project would evolve without being bogged down by slowly moving inventory.

To create the Shelby suspension, Shelby American engineer Ken Miles went to work with two Mustang hardtops. Testing took place at Willow Springs Raceway, where Miles and Bob Bondurant combined the tricks of their driving experience with the existing unibody and various parts already available from Ford. It was understood that using such components would tap a dependable source, facilitate ordering and inventory, and contribute to the bottom line. Miles eventually determined that if Ford's San Jose assembly plant could furnish Fastbacks with Detroit Locker units in Ford 9in rear ends, close-ratio Borg Warner T-10 close-ratio synchronized four-speed transmissions, 9.5in front disc brakes and station wagon rear drum brakes with metallic linings, plus the heavy-duty firewall-to-shock tower V-shaped brace installed on Mustangs destined for export, Shelby could finish the job in Venice, California. As *Motor Trend* pointed out in its first road test of the car, "The words here are: control, limit, locate, stiffen, and snub."

The San Jose cars would be Wimbledon White with black standard Mustang

Clean and mean from the rear, the first-edition Shelby carried detailing right down to the GT-350 badge on the taillight panel. The 1965 GT-350s used a stock Ford Mustang gas cap, though later models would sport Shelby-unique designs.

While a Falcon-type instrument cluster dominates the driver's forward view, the custom wood steering wheel and Cobra logo center cap promise more adventurous action. Early cars received 16in-diameter steering wheels, though most got 15in models. The stock Mustang four-speed shifter handle and knob ride atop a Borg-Warner T-10 transmission.

interiors, and 5.5x15in argent steel wheels as produced for Ford by Kelsey-Hayes. Assembly would delete hoods, hood latches, the "pony and corral" grille bars, Ford and Mustang identifying badges, rear seats, radios, and exhaust systems.

After the first three prototype fastbacks were delivered, built, and approved early in the model year, Shelby American ordered from San Jose enough partially completed, or "knockdown," Mustangs to satisfy both the 100-car homologation rule and the company's anticipated need for racing models. The transformations began. Some changes were quick and clean, while lowering the front upper control arms (for lower center of gravity and to optimize camber changes) or removing the rear axles to install override traction bars were labor intensive. The front suspensions were reassembled using new 1in anti-sway bars, Koni shock absorbers (also added at the rear), and special idler and Pitman arms for improved response and, with a power steering ratio in the steering gear box, less lock-to-lock travel.

The Shelby interior retained the early Mustang's (Falcon style) instrument cluster, standard upholstery, standard door panels, and black carpet. It then received a wood-rimmed Cobra steering wheel (16in steering wheels on the first batch of cars, and 15in wheels on subsequent Shelbys); an instrument pod at the center of the dash-pad, housing a CS custom-logo Delco tachometer and an oil-pressure gauge; a spare tire mounted on the fiberglass deck that had replaced the rear seat; and 3in-wide Ray Brown competition seat belts.

The 271hp Hi-Po engine received only external changes. A 715cfm Holley four-barrel carburetor was mounted upon a cast-aluminum Cobra Hi-Riser intake manifold. Cast-aluminum Cobra-lettered valve covers and an extra-capacity cast-aluminum Cobra-lettered oil pan replaced the stock pieces, and tubular steel Tri-Y exhaust headers led to 2in-diameter Glaspak mufflers and exhaust pipes that exited just ahead of the rear wheels. Still, these simple external changes boosted power, and Shelby advertised his version of the 289ci High Performance engine as having 306hp. For the advantage of weight transfer, batteries were shifted to trunk mountings; due to complaints of fumes and corrosion, this modification was discontinued about half-way through 1965 production. Goodyear's 7.75x15 High Performance Blue Dot tires were mounted on the standard steel wheels or the optional Cragar-built wheels with CS center caps.

Additional modifications included the addition of the following:
- Twin axle limiting cables connecting the rear axle to frame rail-mounted eyebolts
- Driveshaft safety loop affixed to the underside of the front seat belt mounting holes
- Transverse engine compartment "Monte Carlo" bar from shock tower to shock tower
- Dash-mounted horn toggle to replace the one lost in swapping steering wheels
- Fiberglass hood with a working air scoop and Klik pin retainers
- Guardsman Blue GT-350 lower body stripes
- Mustang tri-color bar/running horse fender emblem mounted on the left side of the grille mesh

The Production Line Rolls

The street GT-350s produced by Shelby American caused a stir in the dealer

---

The Carroll Shelby Resumé

- National Driving Champion, Sports Car Club of America (SCCA), 1956 and 1957.
- Named "Sports Car Driver of the Year" by *Sports Illustrated*, 1956 and 1957.
- Won the 24 Hours of Le Mans in 1959 driving with Roy Salvadori in an Aston Martin DBR1.
- National Road Racing Champion, US Auto Club, 1960.
- World Manufacturers Championship won by the Shelby Cobra, 1965.
- Shelby American-prepared Ford GT-40 Mk IIs swept first three places at 24 Hours of Le Mans, 1966.
- Shelby American-prepared Ford GT-40 Mk IV driven by A. J. Foyt and Dan Gurney won 24 Hours of Le Mans, 1967.

The Le Mans up-and-over stripes, ornament-free grille area, side stripes, GT-350 designation, and side-exit exhausts proclaimed the new Shelby Mustang's demeanor.

Cast of Characters

Klaus Arning: Ford Motor Company suspension engineer, who assisted in design of initial GT-350 suspension.

Pete Brock: Shelby American designer, who created "G.T. 350" lower body panel stripes. Shelby's first employee.

Chuck Cantwell: Shelby American GT-350 project engineer. Team driver.

Peyton Cramer: Shelby American general manager, who proposed and closed the deal with Hertz Corporation for the sale of 1,002 1966 GT-350H models. Partner with Carroll Shelby in Hi-Performance Motors, Inc., 1150 South La Brea, Los Angeles.

Al Dowd: Early Shelby American employee. Partner in Hi-Performance Motors, Inc. Managed race teams.

Ken Miles: Shelby American competition director. Engineer and primary development test driver for Shelby GT-350. Won B/Production class at the first race entered by a Shelby GT-350 (5R002), the SCCA Nationals at Fort Worth, Texas, February 14, 1965. Killed August 1966 while testing Prototype J-chassis GT-40 at Riverside.

Jerry Schwartz: Shelby American fabricator and race mechanic. In charge of R-Model construction.

Lew Spencer: Shelby American team driver (Cobras, Tiger, Daytona Coupe). Partner in Hi-Performance Motors, Inc. Shelby American competition sales manager who oversaw the Race Assistance Program. Trans Am team manager, 1967-1969. Returned to Shelby's employ from early 1980s until early 1990s.

Jerry Titus: Shelby American team driver, who won 1965 SCCA B/Production championship in SFM5R001.

The 260 Cobra Impact: Reactions from the Automotive Media

"For those wishing to cause consternation in the hairy big-bore production ranks, the line forms on the right."
—*Sports Car Graphic*, May 1962.

" . . . the airblast at high speeds tends to bend the windshield right back."
—*Car Life*, 1962.

" . . . the AC Cobra attained higher performance figures than any other production automobile we have tested. And it did it with the 'street' engine."
—*Car and Driver*, March 1963.

"Lest there be any doubt as to the effectiveness of the Cobra, be it known that the Miles car had blown an oil hose early in the race, spent time having it replaced, came back to the pits to wait around some more while a flat tire was changed, and still managed to beat Dick Lang's Sting Ray, Tony Denman's Corvette roadster, two more Sting Rays and Al Rogers' ailing Morgan SS."
—*Sports Car Graphic*, December 1963, regarding that year's SCCA GT Class U.S. Road Racing Championship race at Mid-Ohio. Miles came in second to Bob Holbert's Cobra.

In keeping with SCCA competition rules, all 1965 Shelby Mustangs were two-seaters. A fiberglass deck replaced the rear seat, and Shelby American mounted the spare tire on the deck. The naugahyde spare tire cover at left was standard for the GT-350.

Shelby American riveted its own Vehicle Identification Number plate over Ford's inner left fender VIN stamping. The code on this car is SFM5S266; SFM indicates Shelby Ford Mustang, the 5 is the final digit for model year 1965; the S means a street version (as opposed to R for a racing Shelby), and 266 is the consecutive unit number.

1965 Shelby GT-350 Color Chart

Exterior color: Wimbledon White, 1964½–1971 Mustang code M. All GT-350s had Guardsman Blue lower body stripes.
Interior color: Black standard Mustang upholstery and door panels.

Le Mans stripes: Guardsman Blue (Mustang code F). Fewer than 200 cars were shipped from Shelby American with Le Mans stripes; of those, fewer than twenty-five had base steel wheels. Ford dealers were responsible for the application of many additional sets of Le Mans stripes.

GT-350 Engine Specifications

Displacement	289ci ohv V-8
Bore	4in
Stroke	2.87in
Compression ratio	10.5:1
Horsepower	306 at 6000rpm
Horsepower per cubic inch	1.06
Torque	329lb-ft at 4200rpm
Carburetor	Holley 715cfm

GT-350 Body and Frame

Unitized body	Bolt-on front fenders
Wheelbase	108.0in
Track, front	56.0in
Track, rear	56.0in
Overall length	181.6in
Overall width	68.2in
Overall height	52.2in
Curb weight	2,800lb

Ford and Shelby Vehicle Identification Numbers

Because the 1965 Mustang Fastbacks destined for Shelby American came from San Jose with the same engines, their eleven-place 5R09Kxxxxxx VINs were similar. The 5 was for 1965, R designated the San Jose plant, 09 was the fastback body style, K signified the High Performance 289ci engine, and the final six digits pinpointed an individual car's sequence on the assembly line. Mustang VINs were stamped on the inner fenders and on most K-code engine blocks.

Shelby American, as a bona fide manufacturer, assigned its own numbers to each completed GT-350. The VIN form was SFM5Sxxx, with the first three letters for Shelby Ford Mustang, the 5 indicating the 1965 model year, the S for street model (or an R for race model), and three consecutive unit numbers. Shelby stamped their VIN on an aluminum plate attached to the driver's side inner fender (atop the Ford VIN) and on the passenger's side inner fender. On cars 004 through 034, the fifth space in the VIN (for an R or an S) was left blank. After 034 had been completed, the company realized the need for separate designations; prototype cars 001, 002, and 003 were assigned official VINs late in the model year, so the R and the S appear in their codes.

1965 GT-350 Production

Street prototype:	1
Competition prototype:	2
Competition Shelbys:	34
Base price: $5,995.00	
Street models:	516
Base price: $4,547.00	
Drag racing models:	9
Total:	562

Source: 1987 *Shelby American World Registry.*

The Shelby Mustang interior featured a genuine wood steering wheel, the Falcon-style instrument cluster, a dashpad-mounted gauge pod, special Ray Brown 3in seat belts, standard black Mustang upholstery, and the stock Mustang four-speed shifter. Note the stock radio in Shelby 5S266.

The 1965 Shelby grille was the Mustang unit without the chromed pony and wing bars, but with the running horse and vertical tri-color bar emblem found on Mustang front fenders. The stock Mustang hood latch mechanism was removed, and Klik pins through chromed posts secured the fiberglass hoods.

Shelby American was a bona fide manufacturer; thus, their Vehicle Identification Numbers took precedence over Ford's numbers. To cover the factory-stamped Ford VIN, Shelby American riveted its own identification plate at the top inner fender. This remarkable restoration includes vintage heater hoses, the proper fuel pump (with early-style fuel filter), open-letter Cobra valve covers, Koni shocks, and Tri-Y headers. The Monte Carlo bar between the inner fenders and the U-shaped "export" brace connecting the top center firewall to the shock towers strengthened the forward section and helped maintain front end alignment under stress. Ford specified the "export" brace for Mustangs ordered to be shipped out of the country. Presumably, the roads of Europe and South America would put unusual strain on the Mustang unibody.

These days, a winning concours restoration requires incredible details. The new old stock radiator hose and original spark plug wiring are among this car's finer points.

network and production leapt beyond the original target of 100 cars. By March 1965, the small company outgrew its Venice plant and moved to a converted North American Aviation factory on West Imperial Highway, adjacent to the Los Angeles International Airport. The Shelbys also brought much ink to the automotive magazines, and, perhaps too often, caught the attention of law enforcement.

One primary reason for the 1965 Shelby's instant and continuing reputation as a genuine performer is that the only modification Shelby American made strictly for effect was the paint stripe scheme. In most opinions, the eye-catching stripes were tasteful and mindful of the world-class Ford race cars of the day. But every change ordered from Ford and installed by Carroll Shelby's factory personnel during the 1965 model year related directly to improved road-course performance and durability.

Even after all the planning, ordering, and designing, Shelby American remained flexible and open to change. The steering wheels were downsized, then changed. The battery was returned to the engine compartment after problems arose. The hood design was changed to provide steel bracing for the fiberglass. And, toward the end of the model year, California-, Florida-, and New Jersey-bound GT-350s needed rear-exit exhaust systems. Whether brought about by customer input, legal problems, parts availability, or improved performance, changes were swift and positive.

Carroll Shelby worked off a gut philosophy centered on torque, fun, g-forces, and potential profit. Having great employees was also a key. The designers, test drivers, team managers, fabricators, transport drivers, and office employees made up a genuine team. With that help, plus his grass roots manufacturing expertise and ability to charm the automotive media, Shelby was the man for the moment. The 1965 Shelby Mustang proved it.

No matter what Ford thought it needed, Shelby produced the car he wanted. In the beginning, demand for 1965 Shelbys had to grow to match production. The situation quickly turned and, for a while, demand outpaced output. Subsequent years' changes would lead us to believe that Shelby's first version of the specialty Mustang might have been too rough-and-ready for the majority of Ford dealers to market. Today, those premier

To add to the real world performance feel as well as genuine utility, Shelby American installed a custom-crafted dash gauge pod on the 1965 GT-350. The CS logo oil-pressure gauge and tachometer (actually a Delco unit) helped keep costs low because the Falcon-style instrument cluster could remain as installed by the factory.

A shock tower-to-shock tower brace, called a Monte Carlo bar, crosses above the forward section of the Shelby-modified High Performance 289hp engine. Ford's Hi-Po, available in 271hp form in the Mustangs, departed Shelby American now rated at 306hp. Note the fan shroud and missing battery.

Standard for the GT-350 were the heavy-duty station wagon 5.5x15in argent-painted steel wheels with chromed lug nuts. The wheels were subcontracted to Kelsey Hayes and delivered to Ford's San Jose Mustang plant to be installed on the Fastbacks destined for Shelby American.

models are most highly prized. Who was right? Who can say?

The project was right, and no one will argue that fact.

In the beginning, Shelby American mounted the Autolite battery in the right side of the trunk. After receiving owner complaints about fumes and corrosion, the company installed the now-rare Cobra vent caps shown here—but complaints continued. The final forty percent of 1965 GT-350 production found the batteries in the standard underhood location.

Cragar worked from an existing design to accommodate Shelby specs for an optional 6x15in two-piece wheel. Chromed steel rims surrounded aluminum centers with chromed CS logo center caps. The G.T.350 lower side stripes were Guardsman Blue, a 1964½ Mustang exterior color.

"We recommend it as a sure cure for all strains of boredom."

"When you start the [1965 GT-350] engine, you're first impressed with a raucous note from the twin exhausts. They're actually louder *inside* the car, because there's no insulation or undercoating.

"The GT-350, in fact, develops so much cornering force that the idiot light came on and the gauge wavered (it has both) on several occasions due to oil surge in the sump.

"Our best was just under 17mpg when driving at steady legal speeds on freeways. The low, 11.2, came during performance testing. Average for our 900-mile test was 14 mpg."

—*Motor Trend*, May 1965

Shelby GT-350 Competition Models

It's Who's Up Front that Counts

Ford initially failed to convince the SCCA to qualify the Mustang for production class competition. In a second approach, Carroll Shelby became the messenger. After talking shop with John Bishop, executive director of the SCCA, Shelby got the go-ahead for a two-seated sports racer. In order for the cars to qualify as "production" models, Shelby agreed that no fewer than 100 would be built before January 1965. And, based on those limited production cars, the racing version could have either a modified engine or a modified suspension. While the SCCA may have doubted Shelby's ability to build 100 spe-

The real reason for the Shelby GT-350 was to win headlines and boost the image of the 1965 Mustang. While the regular 1965 Shelby was a formidable performance vehicle, the workhorses meant for competition were the thirty-six racing or R-Models built specially by Shelby American for SCCA B/Production battles across the country. Among the weight-shaving measures incorporated in the Shelby R-Models was the elimination of the front bumper and the replacement of the steel valance with a fiberglass front apron. Openings in the apron allowed additional engine cooling, plus the ducting of air to the front brakes. To allow tire clearance, the front fender edges were flattened and the bottom front corner trimmed.

cialty automobiles in a matter of months, it was the Green light Ford needed.

The Shelby Success Formula

Step one was to turn a Mustang Fastback into a production sports car, the "street" Shelby GT-350 with its essentially unmodified and Ford-warranted 289ci Hi-Po engine and its highly modified Shelby American-designed suspension. That car would be reasonably priced and reasonably functional for highway use.

Step two was to build 100 of the cars, a few for racing but the majority for dealer showrooms. Shelby American's Cobra manufacturing facility in Venice, California, would be adapted for that process and, eventually, selected dealerships across the nation would sell the cars.

Step three called for the creation of a race car in compliance with the SCCA's edict regarding the modification of either the engine or suspension. That was easy. By changing a Mustang into a street Shelby, the suspension already was optimized; that left the door open for Shelby American to internally modify the race car engines. Only weeks into production, when the SCCA's representatives inspected the Shelby American plant, they found 100 white fastbacks with blue stripe schemes.

IT'S WHAT'S UP FRONT THAT COUNTS!

When you take half a Mustang and half a Cobra, power it with 306 Ford horses and call it the G.T. 350, you end up with a pile driving powerhouse from Shelby-American that's unbeatable anywhere...on the street or in competition. Take the SCCA Pomona ABC Production race on June 20...first overall. Take Elkhart Lake on the same weekend...first in B, fourth overall (the first three, all A Production, were Cobras). Let's take a look at just a small part of the record.

Kent	Titus	1st overall
Cumberland	Johnson	1st in Bp
Lime Rock	Johnson	1st in Bp
	Donahue	2nd in Bp
	Krinner	3rd in Bp
	Owens	4th in Bp
Willow Springs	Cantwell	1st in Bp
Mid-Ohio	Johnson	1st overall
Dallas	Miles	1st in Bp

G.T. 350 STREET VERSION SPECIFICATIONS Shelby-American prepared 289 cubic inch O.H.V. Cobra V-8 engine equipped with special high riser aluminum manifold, center pivot float four barrel carburetor, hand built tubular "tuned" exhaust system featuring straight through glass-packed mufflers, finned Cobra aluminum valve covers, extra capacity finned and baffled aluminum oil pan; fully synchronized Borg Warner special Sebring close ratio four speed transmission; computer designed competition suspension geometry; one inch diameter front anti-roll bar; fully stabilized, torque controlled rear axle; 6½" wide wheels mounted with Goodyear "High Performance-Blue Dot" tires; Kelsey Hayes front disc brakes; wide drum rear brakes with metallic linings; competition adjustable shock absorbers; integrally-designed functional hood air scoop; competition instrumentation including tachometer; racing steering wheel; rear quarter panel windows; rear brake air scoop; competition seat belts; 19:1 quick ratio steering.

G.T. 350 COMPETITION VERSION Additions to the street version include: Fiberglass front lower apron panel; engine oil cooler; large capacity water radiator; front and rear brake cooling assemblies; 34 gallon fuel tank, quick fill cap; electric fuel pump; large diameter exhaust pipes; five magnesium bolt-on 7" x 15" wheels, revised wheel openings; interior safety group including roll bar; full Shelby-American competition prepared and dyno-tuned engine; every car track-tested at Willow Springs before delivery.

SHELBY G.T. 350

The racing community learned in the November 7, 1964, issue of *Competition Press and Autoweek* that the "Cobra-Mustang" racing effort had been approved for B/Production in 1965.

While the more numerous street Shelbys allowed the marque to be homologated by the SCCA, the competition, or R-Model GT-350s, wrote the headlines. The gunsmoke and tire rubber Ford wanted for its Mustang image campaign, the victories noted at regional tracks and in the national press, and the brain-rattling reputation of the Shelby cars came directly from the race cars. The R-Models came directly from the minds and wrenches of successful competitors and mechanics versed in optimizing the 289ci engines. The GT-350 victories would come from both Cobra team veterans and regional independents.

If San Jose's knockdown models destined to be street GT-350s were devoid of certain parts, the Mustangs headed for R-Model status were downright bare. They were expressly built with the goal of eliminating excess weight. Many things were deleted: steel hoods, hood latches, grille bars, Mustang badges, rear seats, radios, exhaust system, sound deadener, seam sealer and undercoating, window regulators, side glass, backlight, gas tank, door panels, headliner, heater/defroster system, and carpet. The R-Models reached Shelby American at fighting weight. Furthermore, at Shelby American, a lightweight fiberglass apron, ducted for brake and engine cooling, replaced the front bumper, the rear bumper was removed, and thin aluminum panels were riveted over the holes created when the heavy C-pillar air extractor vents were removed.

To replace the missing back and side Carlite glass, pull-up Plexiglas side windows in aluminum frames were installed in the doors and a molded Plexiglas rear window filled the space, saved weight and, with a slot at its forward edge, provided additional ventilation to the interior. All told, nearly 500lb were eliminated in the building of Shelby competition models.

The High Performance 289ci Mustang engines were removed from the R-Models-to-be and dismantled at Shelby American. The heads went to Valley Head Service for porting and polishing, internal components were balanced, and reassembly was done to blueprint specifications. Each four-barrel competition engine received a camshaft that pushed the power curve toward the top end, a fully degreed harmonic balancer, and a 7qt Aviad oil pan, which required a custom-made anti-sway bar.

To keep the engines alive, Shelby modified the oiling system and installed an oversized radiator; an oil cooler was positioned low and just aft of the radiator. A spun-aluminum plenum directed air from

The R-Models could be ordered through the dealer network, though their $6,000 price tag kept many mid-1960s purchasers on the sidelines. In June 1965, Shelby 5R104 was delivered directly to Ford dealer Mack Yates in St. Louis, Missouri, who campaigned his GT-350 with much success throughout the Midwest. For a number of the earlier R-Models, including the one in this photograph, the custom production process included enlarging the rear wheel openings. Perhaps to avoid a rule technicality, this was done in a manner that left the openings looking close to stock. Eventually, a challenge ended the modification, and later R-Models simply had the fender lip rolled and flattened for clearance.

the stock hood scoop to the 715cfm center-pivot Holley. A dual-plane high-rise aluminum intake manifold, large tube headers, a

Stewart-Warner electric fuel pump, and a straight pipe exhaust system topped off the performance R-Model changes. Finally, each R-Model engine was tuned on a dynomometer. Horsepower readings generally registered in the neighborhood of 350.

To deal with the realities of racing, the R-Model GT-350s also received slightly flared and re-radiused wheel openings, 34gal baffled gas tanks (actually two stock Mustang tanks welded together, then painted black), quick-release gas caps fitted with splash collars, gutted dash panels equipped with six CS analog gauges, two lightweight and snug racing seats, 3in competition harnesses, and a four-point rollcage for both rigidity and driver safety.

In spite of the Le Mans and lower body stripes common to the street and race

GT-350s, an R-Model, with its Goodyear Blue Streak 6.00/9.30x15 racing tires, fiberglass rear window and front valance, and American Racing's aftermarket GT model five-spoke 7x15in magnesium wheels, looked much meaner than a standard Shelby. To complete the assembly process, each R-Model was tested by Shelby American company drivers at Willow Springs.

A Winner From the Start

All this preparation was done to win races, and proof of the Shelby success formula came with the debut outing of the first prototype R-Model. A winner popped right out of the box in north Texas when Ken Miles captured a B/Production victory at Green Valley Raceway on February 14, 1965. This success at an SCCA national

From the carburetor plenum to the oversized Modine radiator, an R-Model engine compartment indicated a single purpose: the production of horsepower long enough to win the race. SCCA B/Production rules permitted either engine modifications or suspension upgrades, but not both. Because the production Shelbys had beefy suspensions to begin with, Shelby American opted to boost the horsepower and longevity of the High Performance 289ci engines. An engine block adaptor fed the oil cooler mounted just aft of the radiator. This restored Shelby incorporates every known vintage detail, including cylinder heads reworked and polished by Valley Head Service.

event provided exactly the headline Ford had in mind when the Cobra-Mustang project began. With the pedal to the floorboard, the Shelby GT-350 was off on the right foot.

After the first two racing prototypes were built, R-Models began to be distributed to independent racers throughout the United States, Canada, and Europe. Eventually, several would head for Peru, but the main action happened in the United States. According to Shelby American Automobile Club documents, made public in 1992, thirty-six R-Models—including the two prototypes—were built.

In this more modern era, when new car showroom decisions seem to be limited to color choice and stereo quality, it is astounding to think that in 1965 and 1966, a track-ready car could be ordered from and delivered to dozens of Ford dealerships. The prices of the cars generally ranged from $6,500 to $7,150, at least twice the cost of a street Mustang of the era but, in retrospect, fantastic bargains.

Even today, these Shelby R-Models are regarded as serious racing vehicles. To call them jarring is an understatement: When "seat of the pants" is redefined as "where a driver's butt muscles can detect a broken shock or a rock in the road," you know a race car is eager for action. Except in areas of electronic technology and tires, there are few ways today's vintage racers can improve on the old design.

The Shelby formula for success, invented on the spot for perhaps only a season or two worth of Ford Motor Company advertising claims, for boosting the Mustang image, did more than its task. It has stood the test of time.

The R-Models could have received any of four different sized tires. One of those choices was Goodyear Blue Streak 6.00/9.30x15 tires on 7x15in magnesium American Racing wheels.

GT-350 Drag Cars

According to factory paperwork located by SAAC, nine 1965 and four 1966 GT-350s were built specifically for drag racing. Don McCain, a Shelby American sales representative, conceived of the idea to campaign a Shelby GT-350 at West Coast tracks. Racing fabricator and engine builder Bill Stroppe was asked to help create a car that would be legal for National Hot Rod Association competition.

To protect Shelby American from customer complaints about blown engines, all non-factory racers were delivered with the stock Shelby version of the High Performance 289ci engine. But the rest of a drag GT-350 was designed for a single purpose.

The best time registered by one of these factory drag cars was a 12.68 turned by Gus Zuidema at Lebanon Valley, New York.

Drag unit features included:
Gabriel Silver Eagle 50/50 rear shocks (1965)
Koni rear shocks (1966)
9x14 tires on 5x14 steel wheels (1965)
Casler "cheater slicks" on 15in steel wheels (1966)
5.13:1 gear ratio (1965)
4.86:1 gear ratio (1966)
Engine torque strap (1965)
Belanger drag headers
Cure-Ride 90/10 up-lock front shocks
NHRA-approved Cobra scattershield
Hurst Competition-Plus shifter
Driveshaft safety loop
"AFX" rear traction bars
Heater/defroster delete option (1966)
Aluminum carburetor plenum chamber (1966)
Source: *1987 Shelby American World Registry*

A reunion of R-Model Shelby GT-350s at the SAAC 1989 convention in the Pocono Mountains brought together seven of the original thirty-six race cars.

Road-Racing Finesse

"The Shelbys were primitive by today's standards, but were the most fun car I ever drove. If the car wasn't handling right, you could compensate for it in your driving. Throw it into the corner sideways, manhandle it, almost like driving a dirt track car. They had so much torque that you could get away with a lot. They were a fairly forgiving car, although when you made a mistake, it was usually a big one."

—Dan Gerber

Another method of shaving weight from the competition Shelbys was to eliminate the Mustang C-pillar air vents and rivet simple aluminum plates over the holes.

A Ford GT-40 leads a pack of R-Model GT-350s through a quickly moving parade lap on Pocono's tri-oval track.

SCCA rules permitted the elimination of bumpers to save weight. The Shelby R-Model gas filler inlet was inside the trunk, so a cover plate replaced the stock Mustang inlet. For quick pit stop access to the R-Model filler, a Klik pin replaced the trunk lid lock mechanism.

Only three of the original R-Models are believed to be actively raced in vintage competition. SAAC co-director Rick Kopec enters his Essex Wire GT-350 whenever possible.

Early 1965 GT-350s (perhaps the first 300 units) had trunk-mounted Autolite batteries, but only the R-Models had custom-built 34gal fuel tanks fabricated from two bottom sections of the stock Mustang 16gal tank. Internal baffling helped fuel delivery during high-g action, and the conical splash plenum surrounded a 3in pop-open filler cap. The overflow hose leading from the splash plenum drained through the floor pan; the gas tank vent hose looped upward between the rear window and trunk opening, then forward of the right-side trunk hinge, then inside the upper right rear fender to exit above the right taillight.

Fremont, Michigan, Ford dealer and racing enthusiast Dan Gerber became a successful independent R-Model driver. He would occasionally race as a Shelby team member and, in 1966, qualified for the American Road Race of Champions (ARRC). Note the size of the rear tires and enlarged rear wheel opening on car number 14 (5R099).

Replacing the standard rear glass with a specially molded Plexiglas piece saved 20lb. A 1in opening across its top allowed air to be ducted from the car's interior and blended with the exterior airstream; this was thought to contribute to top speed. Note the rear deck spare tire mounting and a portion of the R-Model rollcage.

R-Model Race Results

All but a handful of the competition Shelbys went to independent racers, and they were responsible for some of the more significant victories and finishes at the time.

In the mid-1960s, the SCCA sponsored regional races throughout the country and, at season's end, held the American Road Race of Champions (ARRC). Only the top three cars in each class from each of the six regions were invited to the ARRC. At the 1965 race at Daytona, ten GT-350s were among the fourteen B/Production cars and two alternates invited. Five of those had won regional championships, and Jerry Titus in the Shelby American team car 5R001 went on to win the national title. Six other R-Models finished in the top ten: Bob Johnson in 5R102, Walt Hane in 5R103, Tom Yeager in 5R094, Marty Krinner in 5R100, Brad Booker in 5R210, and Mark Donohue in 5R105.

The ARRC race, which capped the 1966 season the Sunday after Thanksgiving, saw at least eight GT-350s entered. A red flag stopped the race on the fourth lap when Dan Gerber's 5R099, doing over 100mph, was hit from behind by a Corvette and sent head-on into the pit wall. (Gerber today refers to the incident as setting the World Deceleration Record.) On the restart, it was learned that work had been done to Mark Donohue's 5R105. He was disqualified, along with eventual winner Don Yenko (Corvette), so the 1966 championship went to Walt Hane in 5R103. Also placing in the top six were Fred Van Beuren in 5R108 and Marty Krinner in 5R100.

Eighteen GT-350s were invited to the 1967 ARRC in Daytona. The top four places went to Fred Van Beuren in 5R108, Brad Booker in 5R210, Roger West in 5R538, and Mack Yates in 5R104.

With little support from Ford and with Shelby American gone on to other racing venues, the GT-350s lost ground to the competition in subsequent years.

A mirror under the front suspension provides a view of the 9qt R-Model Aviad oil pan and brake cooling duct. Because the stock crossmember did not clear the special oil pan, each R-Model received a custom-fabricated unit. This steel-tube crossmember, installed during a complete rebuild by Bob Perkins Restoration, was done to exact original specs. The 1in anti-sway bar was standard on all GT-350s, though the inner-fender sound deadener was deleted only for R-Models.

The sturdy R-Model steering wheel presides over the special six-gauge instrument cluster. The race cars also had radio and heater block-off plates and center hump-mounted fire extinguishers. Some had a standard Mustang bucket seat, while others, as shown here, were constructed with a naugahyde-covered lightweight fiberglass racing seat. The glovebox door, carpeting, and complete heater assemblies were deleted.

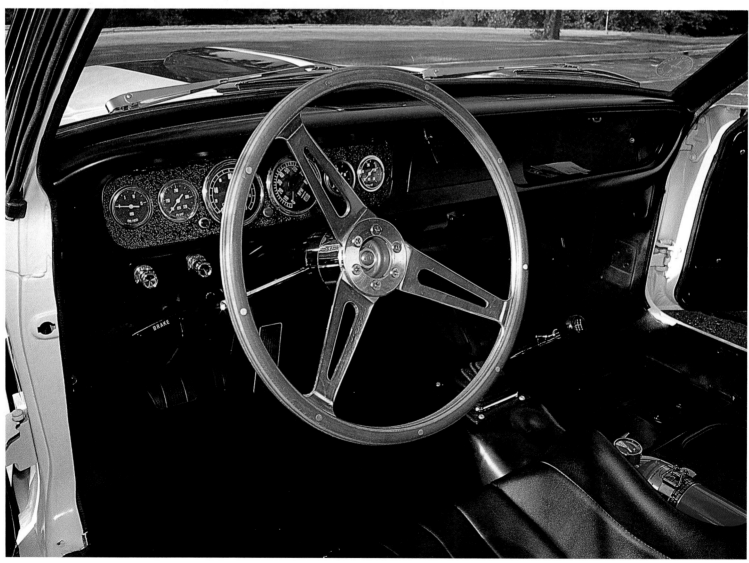

The stock Mustang side glass and window regulators were replaced with weight-saving aluminum-framed plastic side windows with lift straps. A textured aluminum sheet replaces the inner door panel.

1966 Shelby GT-350

The First Restyling.
Sales Quadruple

The 1966 model year became hectic around Shelby American. There were matters of profitability, some "better ideas" from the Ford hierarchy, an anticipated shortage of vehicles available for Shelby while the Mustang plants readied for a new year's production, numerous problems with supplies, and one big surprise: the Rent-a-Racers. What began as a shot in the dark—the attempt to sell Hertz Corporation a handful of GT-350s for more adventurous and well-heeled clients—became a massive interplay between the rental car company and Shelby American. Production for Hertz would end up accounting for forty-two percent of the year's output.

Ford, with its substantial stake in Shelby American, went into 1966 production with a slightly altered viewpoint. Management had viewed the 1965 Shelby GT-350s as effective "loss leaders," a limited number of loud and gutsy image cars that were not, one by one, profitable. But by being seen in competition, in sales literature, and in showrooms, they had done their job of boosting the Mustang's reputation and keeping Mustang sales at record-setting levels. Still, if the program were to continue and grow, a situation closer to profitability was preferred.

At the same time, dealers saw the potential for increased Shelby sales, if only

a few changes were made. If only they had back seats and were slightly less expensive; if only they were quieter, more comfortable, and multi-colored; if only automatic transmissions were offered; and if only they stood out a little more from the standard Mustangs. To the purists, the rough and raw product was fine; to the masses, a little less rough and a lot less raw were needed.

The dealer requests coincided with the recommendations of Ford executives, who had observed the Shelby American operation and had evaluated methods and cost effectiveness. Planning for the 1966 model year began well before production ceased on the 1965 Shelbys. After much discussion, Detroit Locker rear ends, with their odd clunking sounds, became optional, rather than standard, equipment for 1966 Shelbys. Override traction bar instal-

When the promotional aspect of the previous year's Shelby Mustang succeeded, Ford sensed the possibility of profits for the 1966 models. Efforts were made to appeal to an audience broader than the racing enthusiasts who appreciated the first GT-350s. The most obvious change in dealer showrooms was the availability of color combinations other than Wimbledon White with Guardsman Blue stripes.

lation, deemed too time-consuming and therefore too expensive, was reconsidered. After the supply of those units was exhausted (about one-third of the way through 1966 production), Traction Master underride bars sufficed. The 1in drop of the front upper control arms (resulting in a lowered front end and better handling) also took too much hands-on effort and time. Those two changes, when factored out

of the initial Shelby package, were substantial in terms of philosophy as well as performance.

A strange anomaly kicked off the 1966 model year. The Mustang production lines in Metuchen, Dearborn, and San Jose would shut down during approximately the first ten days of August in order to ready themselves for the next year's assembly changes. Because of demand in the distri-

bution and dealer networks, the initial cars off the 1966 lines would necessarily be standard Mustangs. Someone wisely foresaw that Shelby American's supply of partially completed San Jose knockdown models would be interrupted, and Shelby would have few or no cars with which to debut its 1966 GT-350. The solution: As 1965 Mustang production was phased out, 252 chassis—1965 Mustangs intended to be 1966 Shelbys—were shipped from San Jose to the new Shelby American plant in hangars adjacent to the Los Angeles International Airport.

The 252 Wimbledon White carryover vehicles would, in many ways, differ from subsequent 1966 models. They would have some 1965 Mustang characteristics, a good many 1965 Shelby GT-350 details, and many 1966 GT-350 cosmetic changes, including the adaption of the 1966 Mustang grille, Plexiglas C-pillar windows, quarter-panel air scoops, Deluxe Mustang wood-grain-style steering wheel, dash-mounted Cobra tachometer, and Cobra logo GT-350 gas cap.

When the group became completed, the domesticating changes requested by both Ford and its dealer network immediately took effect. Car number 0253 became the first 1966 Shelby based on a 1966 Mustang; it received the first automatic transmission and a true 1966 interior (with updated standard upholstery, inner door panels, and dashpad). Other items found only on the carryover cars were the lowered front upper-control arms, the 1965-style silver painted 15in steel wheels, and Koni shock absorbers (which, along with the Detroit Locker, became a dealer-installed option). Emergency flashers and backup lights first became standard on 1966 Mustangs and so appeared on the post-0252 GT-350s.

All these changes, adaptions to the market, and departures from the race-car nature of the Shelby street models were glimmerings in the crystal ball. The final years of the decade would see a changing Mustang, a more competitive—almost reactionary—pony car market, and the increasing influences of government regula-

If you get lonesome for Italy, eat spaghetti.

We can't knock Ferrari. Nobody can. However, Carroll Shelby, the man who beat Ferrari and brought the world racing crown to America for the first time in history, has taken the '66 Mustang Fastback and designed a car for you. The Shelby G.T. 350 looks like a sports car, drives like a sports car, but has the complete comfort of luxury.

The Pasta. The high-performance 289 Ford engine with four barrel carburetion delivers 306 horsepower. The torque-controlled rear axle, front suspension modifications, and quicker steering provide real handling. The tuned exhaust system makes every-

body sit up and take notice. The four-speed synchronized "stick" (automatic is optional) gives you action when you want it.

The Salsa. The rear quarter panel windows and functional rear brake air scoops, the distinctive grill and hood air scoop, competition instrumentation, steering wheel, seat belts and optional top "Le Mans" stripes and Shelby wheels all add zing to the already racy Mustang.

If you happen to have $13,800, you could buy a Ferrari...or three G.T. 350s and have a little left over for lots of spaghetti.

SHELBY G.T. 350

Here's where you can see, drive, and buy the G.T. 350 • **ALASKA** John Stepp's Friendly Ford, Inc., Anchorage • **ARIZONA** Paradise Ford Sales, Inc., Scottsdale • **CALIFORNIA** McCoy Ford, Anaheim / Webster Ford Sales, Caruthers / Hayward Motors, Hayward / Mark Downing Ford, Inc., Huntington Beach / Mel Burns, Inc., Long Beach / Hi-Performance Motors, Inc., Los Angeles & El Segundo / City Motors, National City / Robert J. Poeschl, Inc., Oxnard / Warren-Anderson Ford, Riverside / Downtown Motors, Inc., Sacramento / Galpin Motors, Inc., San Fernando / S & C Motors, Inc., San Francisco • **COLORADO** Courtesy Motors, Inc., Englewood • **HAWAII** Honolulu Auto Center, Inc., Honolulu • **NEW MEXICO** Richardson Ford Sales, Inc., Albuquerque • **OREGON** Marv Tonkin Ford, Portland 16 • **UTAH** Bennett Motor Company, Salt Lake City.

"If you get lonesome for Italy, eat spaghetti." Much mileage was gained from the Ford-Ferrari rivalry and Ford's victory with GT-40s at Le Mans. Because of Carroll Shelby's input to the GT-40 program, promotional efforts for his products played on Ford's dominance.

tors and insurance industry pressure. The Shelby, too, would change with the times.

Adding Flash to the 1966 Shelby

To differentiate the 1966 Shelby from its predecessor, the designers at Shelby American took steps to add flash and, beyond the scooped hoods and striping scheme, visually separate the GT-350 from its Mustang Fastback brethren. Most obvious were the triangular Plexiglas C-pillar windows and the functional lower rear quarter-panel scoops that ducted air to the rear brakes. Three basic 1966 Mustang colors—Raven Black, Candyapple Red, and Ivy Green—plus Sapphire Blue (a 1966 Thunderbird color called Bright Blue Metallic) also became available after the first 252 cars were made.

The 14in wheels offered on 1966 models moved a step away from 1965's 15in pure utility (painted steel) and the Cragar/Shelby option. The standard wheel became a painted Magnum 500, and an attractive cast-aluminum ten-spoke wheel became optional. Reminiscent of the 1963½ Falcon Sprint V-8s, the 1966 Shelbys had 9000rpm tachometers centered atop the dashpad.

Engines in the 1966 cars were internally unchanged, with only a mid-year change in valve cover design marking their uniqueness. Late in the production year, Shelby American made available the Paxton supercharger factory option that had been tested as early as car 0425 during the 1965 model year and car 0051 in the first weeks of 1966 production. Car 0051 received the only known factory application of GT-350S (for supercharged) side stripes.

To some, the model changeover represented a first-stage devolution of the Shelby Mustang. Compared to anything else out there, the slightly restyled car was tremendously exciting, eye-catching, and powerful. To the hard-core enthusiasts, the concept, with all its "if only" stipulations, had become diluted. Many did their best to

order 1966 GT-350s with the 1965 Shelby in mind: Wimbledon White with no Le Mans stripes, Detroit Lockers, Koni shocks, and a deleted rear seat. Still, things had changed. There was no going back.

Still, Carroll Shelby was an inventive marketer. In coordination with selected Ford franchised dealers, he aggressively promoted a line of Cobra brand speed equipment, from complete high-rev racing engines and ring and pinion gear sets to chrome air cleaners and oil cooler adapter

kits. Shelby Parts and Accessories, working out of the West Imperial Highway plant, advertised for mail order CS/Shelby logo aluminum valve covers, cam and tappet sets, tachometers, intake manifolds, and exhaust headers; one dollar would have bought a respondent the Shelby catalog plus tuning tips and a decal.

Additionally, a subsidiary called Shelby Accessories working out of El Segundo, California, marketed driving gloves, Shelby Cobra logo cuff links, ball

A Cobra Sweat Shirt, finest quality cotton. U. S. made, S, M, L, $3.95
B Cobra Cap, cotton, adjustable, S, M, L, $2.95
C Cobra Windbreaker, blue nylon, concealed hood, S, M, L, $15.95

D Driving Gloves, black leather, chamois-back, $7.95
E Driving Gloves, tan leather, knit-back, $8.50
Made in England.
Men's sizes 7, 7½, 8, 8½, 9, 9½, 10
Women's sizes 6½ & 7

F Gold plated cuff links, $2.95
G Gold plated key chain, $1.25
H Gold plated butane lighter, $4.95

I Cocktail Glasses, set of 4, fired in 23 karat gold, $4.95
J Pilsner Glasses, set of 4, fired in 23 karat gold, $4.95

K-L Coffee or Beer Tankards, white ceramic, fired in 23 karat gold, K (14 oz.), $3.95—L (9 oz.), $3.50
M Cobra Ashtray, white ceramic, fired in 23 karat gold, $3.50

N Shelby-Cobra Helmet, in blue, gray or white, with visor, approved by American Snell Foundation, Sizes 6¾, 6⅞, 7, 7⅛, 7¼, 7½ $29.95
O Pit Stop— A Real Man's Deodorant $1.50

P Cobra Champ T-Shirt, sizes EX S, S, M, L, EX L $1.50

Q GT-350 T-Shirt, sizes EX S, S, M, L, EX L, $1.50

R S T U Shelby-Cobra Racing Illustrations, suitable for framing, 12" x 18", each $1.50, set of 4 $5.00

V Shelby-Cobra Decal, $.25
W Shelby-Cobra Jacket Patch, $1.00

Advertisement for Shelby Accessories, mail order coupon. Perhaps one reason for the immediate and continuing reputation enjoyed by Shelby products was Carroll Shelby's expertise in visionary marketing techniques. The Cobra speed parts business, with Ford's cooperation, spread nationally. Not one to miss a chance, Shelby also authorized the licensing of a broad selection of ancillary items, from posters to deodorant, and beer glasses to driving gloves.

Candyapple Red, Raven Black, Ivy Green, and Sapphire Blue 1966 Shelbys all received white side and Le Mans stripes. In 1966, the GT-350 also incorporated a Plexiglas C-pillar window in place of the Mustang's louvered vents.

Previous page
Because Shelby American's production schedule coincided with Ford's model year change-over, a quantity of 1965 Mustang Fastbacks were shipped from the San Jose plant to Shelby American to be made into 1966 Shelbys. The first 252 GT-350s produced for 1966 were made from that carryover 1965 inventory. The 1966 Shelby grille is the 1966 Mustang grille without a center "pony and corral" ornament.

caps, windbreakers, T-shirts, sweatshirts, beer and cocktail glasses, mugs, ashtrays, jacket patches, decals, artists' prints of racing scenes, Snell-approved driving helmets, and the capper, the renowned Pit Stop, "A Real Man's Deodorant!"

For a period of time, Shelby even succeeded in having his accessory product line included in the catalogs of both Sears and J.C. Penney.

Included among the 2,380 Shelbys constructed for 1966 were six convertibles, essentially an end-of-production special order for Carroll Shelby. Produced in six different colors—Springtime Yellow, Candyapple Red, Ivy Green, blue, Wimbledon

White, and pink—they all had stock Mustang air conditioning with underdash evaporators. As can best be determined, all had ten-spoke wheels, except the red convertible which had 14in Magnums. With Vehicle Identification Numbers ending in 2375 through 2380, these were the only Shelby convertibles created during the 1966 production year. Since then, on two occasions, additional groups of convertibles, created essentially from used Mustang convertibles, have received Carroll Shelby's blessings. No matter how they are judged now and in the future, they are not to be confused with the six original, San Jose-sourced K-code convertibles built by Shelby American.

The complex details needed for proper restoration include the correct distributor, plug wires, and heater hoses, and the numerically coded fuel filter.

The interior of an early 1966 carryover car combines 1965 and 1966 characteristics. The 3in seat belts appeared in both years, though the Ray Brown versions were replaced during 1966 production by those of another vendor. The black standard upholstery, door panels, dashpad, glovebox, and standard interior-style GT instrument bezel are from 1965. Later 1966 Shelbys used the standard 1966 Mustang five-gauge bezel. The dashpad-mounted tachometer for 1966 replaced the previous year's gauge pod. The steering wheel in this Shelby is a woodgrain Mustang Deluxe interior component with a Cobra logo insert. Its chromed center cap is from a Fairlane and does not have Ford Mustang lettering. The biggest interior difference from 1965 was the retention of the Mustang rear seat that all but the first few 1966 Shelbys received.

It is the lucky restorer who locates an unused, original Hi-Po air filter.

The Shelby version of Ford's 289ci Hi-Po remained basically unchanged from 1965 and, with the Shelby-specific Hi-Rise Cobra intake manifold and Tri-Y headers, claimed 306hp. Hollow-letter Cobra valve covers are shown here, though a minor running change was later made in valve cover style. The Monte Carlo transverse bar and heavy-duty "export" firewall-to-shock tower brace were standard for both years. Note the orange Koni shocks, standard on this and all carryover cars and optional for the remainder of the 1966 production year. The carryover cars also had black engine blocks, while later 1966 Shelbys had blue engines, and the carryover 1966 GT-350s had 1965-style fuel pumps with integral filter cannisters. Later cars had standard fuel pumps and their in-line filters screwed directly into the Holley carburetors.

Shelby trunks remained basically identical to the Mustang's. Like many early 1966 Shelbys—carryovers and a few regular production cars—this has no taillight panel GT-350 emblem. The spare wheel matches this Shelby's Cragar wheels.

After test-fitting Shelby #6S051 with a proto-type Paxton supercharger, Shelby American made the Paxton available as a factory-installed option for the remainder of the year.

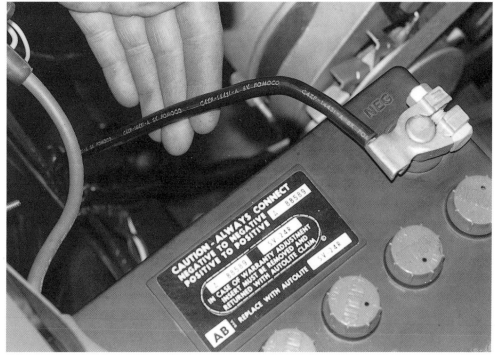

Even the battery and battery cables must have Ford's original part numbers to be correct in today's concours world.

The Cobra logo GT-350 gas cap was standard throughout the 1966 production year.

The Shelby taillight panel emblem was used throughout 1965 but, for some reason, the first 300 or so 1966 GT-350s did not get them. Their installation was resumed, and continued through the end of 1966 production.

In the later months of 1966 production, the 14in Magnum 500 (Motor Wheel), painted gray, with a Cobra/GT-350 logo center cap, became standard. The chromed Magnums were fairly standard for Hertz cars and were found on some regular-production Shelbys.

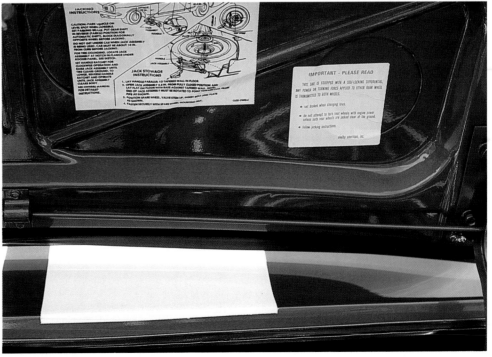

In addition to Ford's Mustang jacking instructions, the underside of the Shelby deck lid carried a warning label regarding the Detroit Locker differential. Because not all owners were satisfied with the Detroit Locker for daily use, it was made a dealer-installed option for 1966.

An optional 14in cast-aluminum ten-spoke wheel was made available during the 1966 production run.

The fine touch in restoration requires duplicating the factory's inherent imperfections, such as the undercoat spray on the firewall slopping over to the heater hoses.

The six Shelby convertibles built at the end of the 1966 production run were produced in six different colors. The cars were not made available to the dealership network, but were presented by Shelby American to special employees and associates. They received the standard Shelby fiberglass hoods and side scoops, the grille treatment, racing mirrors, and emblems.

Previous page
While most of the 1966 Shelby convertibles had cast-aluminum ten-spoke wheels and automatic transmissions, this Candyapple Red GT-350 has chromed 14in Magnum 500 wheels and a four-speed. It is, quite simply, one of a kind.

This is not just a Mustang convertible with a racing mirror, hood scoop, and optional Cobra GT-350 wood rim wheel.

The six special convertibles were the only early Shelbys to have had trunks of this size. Note the Cobra logo gas cap and GT-350 taillight panel badge.

1966 Shelby Color Chart

Color Name	1966 Mustang Color Code	Ditzler Number	DuPont Number
Wimbledon White	M	8378	4480
Raven Black	A	9300	88
Ivy Green	R	43408	4611
Candyapple Red	T	71528	4737
Sapphire Blue	G[1]	13075	4735

[1]1966 Thunderbird Bright Blue Metallic. Not a Mustang color.
1966 Shelby GT-350 interiors were standard black vinyl.

1966 Shelby GT-350 Retail Price List

Shelby GT-350	$4,428.00
High-performance Ford automatic transmission	n/c
Fold-down rear seat	50.00
AM radio	57.50
Alloy wheels	275.00
Rally stripe	62.50
Detroit Locker	141.00
Paxton/Cobra supercharger	670.00

1966 GT-350 Applications, Options, and Exceptions

Lower body stripes: Wimbledon White cars received blue stripes; others received white stripes. Hertz cars received gold stripes (except for several early Wimbledon White-with-blue combinations). Either GT-350 or GT-350H was inset at the lower front fender. All other colors received white stripes.

Le Mans stripes: The over-the-top "rally" stripes, generally dealer-installed, matched the lower body stripes. Most GT-350H cars received Le Mans stripes.

Hoods: Steel-framed fiberglass hoods predominated, with a few mid- and late-production cars receiving all-steel hoods. Attempts to convert to all-steel were plagued with supplier quality control problems.

Wheels and tires: Carryover vehicles received the 1965 choices of silver-painted steel wheels (15x5.5 Ford station wagon units with chrome lug nuts) or 15x6 five-spoke Cragar/Shelby aluminum wheels with chrome CS logo diecast aluminum center caps.

Standard for 1966 was a gray-painted 14in Magnum 500, with 14in aluminum-alloy Shelby ten-spoke wheels optional. Hertz cars received either chromed Magnum 500s or the ten-spoke style with, in most cases, Hertz logo center caps.

Interiors: A single Cobra tachometer replaced the previous year's two-gauge dashpod. The dished Mustang Deluxe woodgrain steering wheel carried a Cobra GT-350 logo in a chromed Fairlane center cap. The 1966 Mustang dashpad, door panels, upholstery pattern, and glovebox appeared after the carryover run of 252 1965-based models.

Traction bars: Shelby American's stock of override bars held through the manufacture of approximately 800 cars. Underride bars predominated after that point.

The standard Mustang upholstery and black-finish instrument bezel and glovebox door do not accurately tell the story. The optional Shelby steering wheel, air conditioning, dash-mounted tachometer, disc brake pedal pad, four-speed shifter, Hi-Po choke lever, and power top switch tell a stronger tale. Note the 00001.0 odometer reading, fresh out of Concours Restorations.

Previous page
The 1966 convertibles' engine compartments differed from the regular GT-350s only in the installation of air conditioning. Only these six special cars received that extra touch directly from the Shelby American factory.

The detailed restoration of the Candyapple Red Shelby convertible included the finer touches of original wiring, starter solenoid, battery, and battery cable.

Many production details were ignored by enthusiasts in the beginning. As time goes by and concours efforts intensify, more is being learned about restoration details, regarding obscure driveshaft and differential bare metal finishes, component paint schemes, and paint daub codes. Note the date-coded Ford Motor Company mufflers, properly tagged differential housing, and Koni shocks.

The Cobra brand 9000rpm tachometer for 1966 replaced the dash-mounted 1965-style tachometer and oil-pressure gauge cluster.

Such details as underbody primer, the proper amount of exterior color overspray, the correct Shelby exhaust system, original convertible underbody brace, grommets, wiring, cables, and natural metal finishes must be extensively researched for restoration.

The 1966 Shelby grille was a 1966 Mustang unit without the "pony and corral" chromed center ornament. The standard Mustang fender emblem is positioned to the left side of the "egg crate" aluminum grille. Note the hood latch pin, Monte Carlo bar, and parts of the air conditioning system in the background. This could only be a Shelby convertible.

The ultimate open-air driver's seat, with the optional Shelby steering wheel and its GT-350 center hub, the Cobra tachometer, radio, air conditioning, a disc brake pedal pad, four-speed shifter, racing-style exterior rear view mirror and, out front, the hood scoop in Candyapple Red. This particular convertible is the only car ever produced that could legitimately have all these extras.

The discrete touch of a Cobra-lettered and finned aluminum extra-capacity oil pan adds to the muscle image of the GT-350.

1966 Shelby GT-350H - The Rent-a-Racers

America Takes the Ultimate Test Drive

If it hadn't been for the Hertz Corporation, Shelby American might have only tripled its output in 1966. Instead, with two prototypes and another 1,000 units going to the rental car concern, Shelby more than quadrupled the GT-350 sales tally of 1965.

In a spirited marketing move, Hertz already had formed the Hertz Sports Car Club so presumably adult and responsible renters might add a little spice to their business trips or weekend breaks. For $17 a day or $70 per week (in the New York area), plus 17 cents per mile, anyone with a proven ability to locate the steering wheel and all of the pedals could sign his or her name and drive away.

To most Hertz clients, it amounted to borrowing a personal race car. Naturally, legend grew from certain truths. More than a few of the rental units ventured toward drag strips and road-racing tracks to become, if not always competitors, prime parts donor cars. Some competed and certainly most were abused on the highway. Years later, general concern about the condition, upkeep, and maintenance of the old rental units caused them to suffer in reputation and value. That suffering screeched to a halt in the late 1970s and early 1980s, and the cars are held today in the same high regard as their private original-owner counterparts.

The performance rental concept had begun with Hertz's program to offer customers Corvettes. So when Shelby American General Manager Peyton Cramer, in September 1965, proposed the sale of a limited number of GT-350s, street versions of that year's B/Production champion, Hertz listened. The corporation's next step, a shock to Shelby American, was to indicate its intent to order 100 models to be called GT-350H (for Hertz) and to incorporate certain minor changes for driver convenience and safety. The news sent Shelby planners scrambling, and during that period Peyton Cramer continued with his correspondence and negotiations.

A prototype car was requested by Hertz on October 26 and, on November 2, the rental company ordered a December delivery of 100 black cars with gold (Bronze Powder) stripes. The cars would be

The Hertz Corporation gave many future Shelby owners their first test drives. Available to members of the Hertz Sports Car Club, presumably clients of maturity and financial substance, the special Shelbys could be leased at more than fifty major airport locations, nationwide. The 1,000 vehicles created for Hertz amounted to better than forty percent of Shelby American's 1966 output.

Approximately 800 Hertz cars were black, and the remaining 200 or so received the standard white, red, blue, and green 1966 Shelby colors. All of the black rental cars had gold side and Le Mans stripes. It is thought that a few early white cars had blue striping, and that few of the non-black cars had Le Mans stripes. Of course, with Shelby American, like Ford, exceptions to the norm were common; for Hertz cars, because of production running changes, there simply was no norm. Note the 1966 Shelby gas cap.

priced at $3,547 f.o.b. St. Louis—a central location—plus $45.45 for a Shelby-installed radio. Shelby American also offered Hertz Corporation a guaranteed depreciation rate which, in the end, amounted to a sort of buy-back program.

On November 9, Hertz requested an automatic transmission version prototype.

It was shipped to Hertz headquarters in New York and, by the end of November, the collaboration had ratcheted up another notch: Hertz increased its order to 200 cars.

According to files found in the mid-1980s in Carroll Shelby's storage areas (and related in the 1987 *Shelby American World Registry*), a series of meetings ensued, during which Hertz and Shelby American planned a joint advertising effort for major print media—automotive and otherwise. Hertz capped the deal by promising, if the $300,000 ad effort received approval, to order another 800 1966 Shelbys. The official order, for a total of 1,000 GT-350s, arrived in late December.

By December 21, Shelby American knew that the first 200 units would be black with gold stripes and that the subsequent

800 units would be built in a variety of Shelby's 1966 color options. What had begun as a longshot sales call evolved into what would become forty-two percent of Shelby American's assembly efforts for 1966. And Shelby GT-350s, unknown to the nation twelve months earlier, suddenly would appear at more than fifty airport rental facilities, Hertz Sports Car Club Centers, coast to coast.

Rent-a-Racers

Both Ford and Shelby are noted for having built cars that were exceptions to the norm. Hertz car production saw similar irregularities. In general, the GT-350Hs had chromed versions of the standard 14in 1966 Shelby Magnum 500 with Goodyear

This front fender detail shows the significant differences between the standard Mustang and the Hertz cars. The functional hood scoop, hood tie-down pin and attaching wire, regal gold Le Mans striping, and the Hertz center cap on the chrome Magnum wheel all contribute to the special image Hertz desired.

Blue Streak tires, radios with front fender-mounted antennas, and, after the first eighty-five units were built, automatic transmissions. Records located and evaluated by the Shelby American Automobile Club indicate that a number of Hertz cars were delivered with cast-aluminum ten-spoke wheels and that approximately seventy-five percent of the cars were black with gold stripes. It is believed that, late in the model year, some cars were delivered with Autolite 595cfm four-barrel carburetors.

One significant problem with the rental units was the difficulty customers encountered with unboosted metallic-lined brakes. After much testing, Shelby American began to install MICO "piggy-back" master cylinders made by Minnesota Automotive. These boosters, which worked in conjunction with the existing master cylinders, led to their own set of problems due to great inconsistencies in brake pedal pressure from unit to unit.

Shelby American had its hands full in producing 1,000 of these cars. For that reason (and because no one thought at the time that car-by-car details would be needed twenty-five or more years into the future), records of running changes, production line exceptions, and parts installed for assembly line expediency are scattered and confusing. Owners and prospective owners needing details on Hertz car characteristics (the information could be its own book) are encouraged to contact SAAC.

Although there is correspondence that indicates a Shelby/Hertz project was discussed for 1967, the end of 1966 production brought the deal to a close. At that point, the repurchase clause concerning guaranteed depreciation brought pressure on Shelby American and Ford to dispose of the Hertz cars being retired from active rental. As John Craft noted in the September 1990 *Mustang Monthly*, a Ford employee named Marv Neely won a contest (called the Visibility 500) to sell the greatest number of ex-Hertz vehicles. Neely and his colleagues are to be credited with saving numerous GT-350Hs from less-noble circumstances.

In retrospect, the Hertz cars, today referred to as Rent-a-Racers, provided Shelby American with genuine traction in the world of commerce. A deal of that magnitude carries its own legitimacy, and the reputation of the small California-based manufacturer grew beyond the increased exposure and production. It provided a fine chapter in the history of Carroll Shelby's manufacture of automobiles.

Hertz is Number One in the minds of hundreds of current Shelby owners. This placard, probably from the early 1980s, is great for display. Collectors constantly search for true vintage artifacts, such as rental counter price lists, color postcards, and old four-fold brochures. Oddly, Hertz considered the 1966 rental program less than successful. In promoting the air conditioned, automatic transmission GT-350s offered to Hertz Sports Car Club members in 1968, the company offered apologies for having previously offered cars that not "everyone" could drive.

Prior to effective sleuthing in recent years by Shelby enthusiasts, it was thought that one could confirm a Hertz model's identity by checking for a steel hood. Perhaps only 150, if that, actually received an all-steel hood; generally speaking, Hertz cars, like regular 1966 Shelbys, used steel-reinforced fiberglass hoods with the functional Shelby scoop.

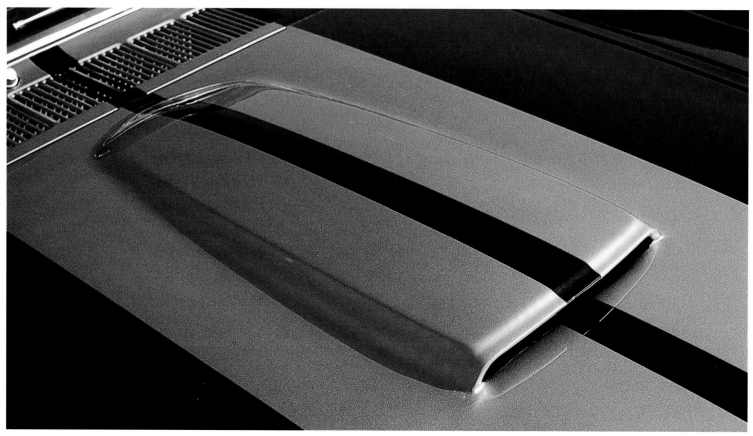

Like regular 1966 Shelbys, the Hertz cars had standard black Mustang upholstery, 3in front seat belts, front disc brakes (note pedal pad), and dash-mounted tachometers. Early GT-350Hs had four-speed transmissions, but over 900 came with an automatic transmission, as shown. All had radios and rear seats. The sticker positioned underneath the radio (also found on the dash pad above the radio) warned rental drivers that the "competition" brakes might require higher-than-normal pedal pressure. A few years ago, the Montana-based owner of this car had Carroll Shelby autograph and date the glovebox door.

Hertz specified unique gold and red corporate decals for the wheel center caps that most, but not all, cars received. The rental company also requested that Shelby American add an H to the side stripe GT-350 designation. Chromed 14in Magnum 500 wheels were most common on the GT-350H models, though cast-aluminum ten-spoke and Cragar/Shelby five-spoke wheels also were found on the 1,000 original Rent-a-Racers.

For a period of time early in Hertz car production, the 1966 Shelby colors Wimbledon White, Ivy Green, Sapphire Blue, and Candyapple Red were used. With the exception of a handful of white cars, the non-Raven Black cars received gold Hertz GT-350H side stripes but no Le Mans stripes.

Road Test: Shelby Mustang GT-350H

"Good things do come for the driver of a GT-350. Its cornering ability is a lovely mixture of the beast getting the better of you and you keeping hold of the tiger's tail."
—*Car and Driver*, May 1966

Acceleration

0-30mph	2.1sec
0-40mph	3.1sec
0-50mph	4.9sec
0-60mph	6.6sec
0-70mph	8.9sec
0-80mph	10.8sec
0-90mph	14.2sec
0-100mph	17.9sec

Standing quarter-mile	93mph in 15.2sec
Top speed, observed	117mph
Temperature	51F
Altitude	83ft above sea level

Engine

Type	Water-cooled V-8, cast-iron block, five main bearings
Bore and stroke	4.00x2.87in
Displacement	289ci; 4727cc
Compression ratio	10.5:1
Valve gear	Pushrod-operated ohv, solid lifters
Power (SAE)	306bhp at 6000rpm
Torque	329lb-ft at 4200rpm
Specific output	1.05bhp per cubic inch
Usable rpm range	800-6000rpm
Electrical system	12volt, 55amp-hr battery
Mileage	6-12mpg
Range on 16gal	96-192 miles

Drivetrain

Transmission	Three-speed automatic
Final drive ratio	3.89:1

Chassis
Platform steel frame, semi-integral steel body

Wheelbase	108.0in
Track	Front, 57.0in; Rear, 57.0in
Length	181.6in
Width	68.2in
Height	51.2in
Ground clearance	5.3in
Curb weight	2,884lb
Test weight	3,158lb
Weight distribution	52% front, 48% rear
Pounds per bhp (test)	10.9

Suspension

Front	Independent, upper wishbone, lower control arm and drag strut, coil springs, anti-sway bar
Rear	Rigid axle, semi-elliptic leaf springs, trailing arms

Brakes

Front	11.3in Kelsey-Hayes discs
Rear	10x3in drums, 408sq-in swept area

Steering

Type	Recirculating ball
Turns, lock to lock	4
Turning circle	40ft

Tires   7.75x15 Goodyear Blue Streaks

"Incidentally, the 'H' might well stand for 'Homologated' if Shelby—or, for that matter, Hertz—wanted to race the car as a Group 2 sedan; the 1,000 examples Shelby will produce for Hertz fulfill the FIA's minimum production requirement."
Source: *Car and Driver*, May 1966.

1967 Shelby GT-350 and GT-500

New Styling for the Road Cars

With its roof-mounted and quarter-panel air scoops, an extended nose, and an upswept, spoilered tail, the 1967 Shelby looked like no other automobile on the highway. The cars succeeded in evoking the image of the Ford GT-40s which had won Daytona and dominated the 1966 24 Hours of Le Mans. The center grille-mounted high beams, the wide wind-split hood scoop, the roofline, which, unlike the earlier Shelbys, swept to the rear of the trunk, and the wide, clean taillights, helped separate the GT-350s and GT-500s from all others, especially the standard Mustang.

Competition was evolving in the classes that team cars and GT-350 independent racers had dominated in prior years. The headlines had been won, the victories logged, the image created. Much had changed, and much of the philosophy and strategy behind the new cars would come from Ford and its dealer network. Hot off the sales success of 1966, growth became foremost in their plans. The re-designed Mustang presented a slightly larger and heavier car to Shelby American, and that certainly inspired the designers to take the next generation Shelby a step further.

"The Road Cars"

In line with the concept of pleasing a broader segment of the car buying public,

1967 found many of the previous years' rough edges smoothed by additions of luxury touches: the Mustang Deluxe interior, power steering, power brakes, optional air conditioning, and twice as many exterior colors. Even the premier dealer brochure promoted the Shelbys as "The Road Cars." Still, changes such as the GT-500's 428ci engine option, the progressive rate springs, and the standard rollbar (a first for any production car, as were the shoulder harnesses actuated by rollbar-mounted inertia reels) kept the Shelby in a league of its own. Though the power steering system interfered with its 1965-1966 type steel tube headers, the GT-350 retained the race-proven Shelby-tweaked High Performance 289 engine. The more restrictive Mustang Hi-Po manifolds were used, and probably cost some horsepower.

An article in the February 1967 *Car and Driver* gives credit for the fiberglass

Lime Gold became a popular color in 1967, as did the optional Kelsey-Hayes MagStar wheels. This would be the final year that a High Performance 289ci engine would power the GT-350. The unique C-pillar air extractor scoops added a distinctive touch to the Shelby exterior.

Summer Place

What better way to get there—or anywhere—than a
Shelby GT? Pleasure begins the second you turn the key and bring
alive America's answer to Europe's finest GT cars.

Let your Shelby dealer deliver the goods . . .
and save enough to rent a summer place, buy a boat—
or just chuckle all the way to the bank.*

 **SHELBY G.T.** *350 and 500* **The Road Cars** Powered by

Shelby American, Inc., 6501 W. Imperial Highway, Los Angeles 90009

*GT 350: $3995 Manufacturer's suggested retail price. Includes Cobra 289
CID 306 h.p. V-8, dual exhaust, competition-based front and rear suspensions,
4-speed transmission, h.d. rear, full instrumentation, safety bar, exclusive GT
styling. GT 500 with dual quad Cobra 428 CID V-8, just $200 more. Options, ac-
cessories, delivery, dealer preparation, state and local taxes, additional.

"Summer Place" advertisement for 1967
GT-350 and GT-500. The pleasures of highway
driving were promoted for The Road Cars for
1967. Only two years after the Shelby pitch
touted nothing but performance, Ford's eye had
shifted to a broader market. The "good life"
certainly would include an A-frame summer
house and a quick car to get you there.

Next page
This GT-350 has the standard 1967 wheel
covers: 1967 Thunderbird covers with Shelby
center medallions. In addition to Brittany Blue,
shown here, Shelby American also offered
Bronze Metallic, Dark Blue, Raven Black, Candyapple Red, Wimbledon White, Dark Moss
Green, Medium Metallic Gray, Lime Gold, and
Acapulco Blue. Shelby taillights for 1967 were
1967 Cougar units, and the Shelby-specific gas
cap was a pop-open unit.

The 1967 Shelby, with its jutting grille opening, Le Mans stripes, and center-mounted high beams, looked more menacing than its predecessors. It certainly could not be confused with a mere Mustang.

body panels to Chuck McHose, a Ford stylist who worked closely with Shelby American. In addition to helping distinguish the GT-350s and GT-500s from standard and GT model Mustang Fastbacks, the fiberglass pieces saved weight. Though the stock Mustang front bumper was mounted to stock support braces, the fiberglass Shelby hood measured almost 4in longer than a Mustang's.

The pin-secured hood (which also used a standard-type hood latch) mated to a one-piece fiberglass nose that replaced the front fender extensions, grille surround, gravel pan, and lower valance. The grille-mounted high beams were positioned at

the center until it was learned that certain states, including California, had statutes mandating minimum distance between headlights. Cars headed for those states started receiving lights at the outboard edges of the grille. Legend has it that, in Pennsylvania, one lawmaker who had counted on the purchase of a Shelby with inboard lights actually initiated a change in the state law to accommodate his wish.

The fiberglass roof air extractor worked with an interior vent that could be opened or closed, and the first 200 or so 1967 Shelbys had small red running lights installed in the outflow of the C-pillar scoop. Activated by the brake pedal, the lights were deleted from the production run after those, too, were found to conflict with laws in several states. The lower quarter-panel air scoops fed fresh air, on most early cars, to the rear brakes.

At the rear, the spoiler effect of the fiberglass deck lid was matched by fender

extensions, and wide 1967 Cougar taillights were split by a Shelby-specific pop-open gas cap. Special Shelby tailpipe extensions were routed through the partial cutaways in a 1967 Mustang GT-style lower valance. Again, a stock Mustang bumper was used.

Shelby exterior emblems included identical grille and deck lid nameplates, front fender badges, and lower body panel stripes, all specific to either the GT-350 or GT-500. Shelby emblems also appeared on gas caps and wheel centers. The base wheel for 1967 was a 15in steel one with a Shelby logo 1967 Thunderbird wheel cover. The $185 Shelby wheels offered to purchasers of 1967 models were Kelsey-Hayes 15x7 MagStar units (at only $151.74 on one owner's original invoice) and, later in the model year, the 15in ten-spoke cast-aluminum wheel was offered.

The Deluxe Mustang interior, in either black or Parchment vinyl (with a few white interiors produced as well), included an

Shelby taillights for 1967 were 1967 Cougar units, and the Shelby Cobra gas cap, specific to either the GT-350 or GT-500 models, was a pop-open unit.

1967 Shelby Color Chart

Unlike any Mustang, the 1967 Shelby had its original exterior color noted in the Shelby American-assigned VIN. A numeral located seven positions from the left provided the color code. The letter to the right of the color code numeral indicated the color of the Deluxe interior: A indicated black and U indicated either Parchment or white. The first eighty-nine cars produced did not have the interior code in their VINs.

The first five colors were the only ones scheduled for September build by Report II of the 1967 Prototype Program. Red, gray, and Lime Gold began appearing after car 0099; Brittany Blue started appearing with car 0288; and Acapulco Blue was not a scheduled color until the final third of production.

Color Number	Color Name	1967 Mustang Color Code	DuPont Number	Ditzler Number	R-M* Number
1	Bronze Metallic	V	4793	22749	
2	Dark Blue	K	4780	13076	A-1780
3	Raven Black	A	88	9000	
4	Wimbledon White	M	4480	8378	A-1633
5	Dark Moss Green	Y	4788	43567	A-1879
6	Metallic Gray	4**	4733	32520	
7	Lime Gold	I	4790	43576	A-1882
8	Brittany Blue	Q	4813	13619	A-1643
9	Candyapple Red	T	4737	71528	A-1782R
0	Acapulco Blue	D	4857	13357	A-1935

*R-M stands for Rinished-Mason, the brand of paint generally used on Shelbys made in the San Jose plant. Generally, later-model Shelbys were painted with Ditzler.

**Metallic Gray, termed "Special Dark Metallic Gray #1900 (1967 Thunderbird Only)" in the 1967 GT-350 Prototype Program Report II, also has been called Medium Gray Metallic and Dark Gray Metallic. It was the only 1967 Shelby color that was not a Mustang color for that model year.

Early-production 1967 Shelbys were fitted with C-pillar scoop running lights. Due to legal problems in some states, including California, the state of manufacture, the lights were phased out of production after the first 200 or so cars were completed.

"Everybody looks at you" ad for 1967 GT-350 and GT-500. The elements of luxury and prestige are foremost in this appeal to consumers. Along with "zesty" performance, handling, and brakes, the ad pushes safety and comfort. It would seem that winning races has become secondary to winning friends.

Next page
"Big Stuff" print ad for Shelby Parts Company mail order. The Shelby operation continued to market high-performance bolt-on parts for all Ford enthusiasts. Here, the Shelby Parts Company, an offshoot of Shelby American, promotes speed equipment for big-block engines. The ad copy overflowed with imagination: Here was your chance to own a "Le Mans Kinetic Superflow Solid Lifter Camshaft Kit."

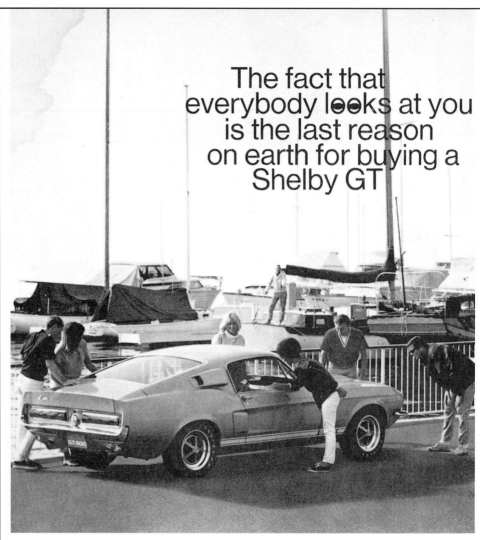

8000rpm tachometer, aluminum insets for the dash area and door panels, an "optional" fold-down rear seat, and deluxe lap belts to accompany the harnesses. The unique wood-rimmed steering wheel and a set of underdash gauges for oil pressure and amperes (fitted to an upside-down early Mustang Rally-Pac) topped off the performance touches.

A Winning Compromise

There were old arguments that be-cause the Mustang was upsized for 1967,

the 1967 Shelby, with its power steering and such, had gained too much bulk to be competitive. With fifty-seven percent of its weight on the front wheels, the GT-500 probably was not destined for road-racing glory, but the SCCA rulebook kept the GT-350s from B/Production competition more than any inherent factor.

Certainly, the size of the cars didn't bother the 1967 Mustang hardtops competing in that year's SCCA A/Sedan series and winning the Trans-Am Sedan Manufacturers Championship. (Ironically, when Ford elected to support the Mustang race cars, it turned to Shelby American for behind-the-scenes expertise.) The true rea-

AT LAST BIG STUFF FOR BIG FORD ENGINES

352 · 390 · 406 · 427 · 428

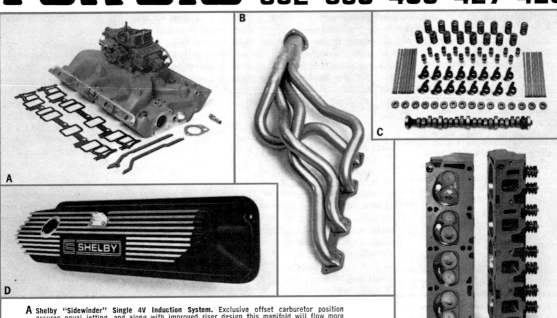

A **Shelby "Sidewinder" Single 4V Induction System.** Exclusive offset carburetor position assures equal jetting, and along with improved riser design this manifold will flow more fuel air mixture than any other 4V in use. Induction kit with 715 cfm Holley carburetor **$230.00.** Manifold only **$145.00.**

B **"Tuned" Headers.** Features tube diameter and routing for maximum horsepower and torque. Headers, extension, gaskets and bolts **$140.00.**

C **LeMans Kinetic Superflow Solid Lifter Camshaft Kit.** Best value in the high performance market. Kit, as shown above, will produce fantastic horsepower ratings in your race modified engine **$140.00.** Camshaft and lifters only **$90.00. Hydro-thrust Hydraulic Camshaft Kit $85.00.**

D **Shelby Aluminum Valve Covers:** Kit includes gaskets, bolts and instructions; internal baffles and breather tube already installed, **$37.95.**

E **Competition Drag Cylinder Heads.** Fully ported and polished with high rev competition valve springs and aluminum retainers.

 **SHELBY**

PARTS AND ACCESSORIES *THE PERFORMANCE LINE*

Ready for drag-strip action, this big-block Wimbledon White GT-500 runs center headlights and 15in cast-aluminum Shelby ten-spoke wheels with slicks mounted at the rear. The 428ci engine was capable of delivering impressive straight-line performance, though road racers felt that the engine's weight diminished overall handling.

son for the Shelby's exclusion went back to its original homologation: The class called for a two-seater, and the 1967 Shelby clearly had four seats.

For 1967, Carroll Shelby was forced to rethink his approach and blend it with Ford's intentions. But once again, Shelby American created and produced an eye-

and ear-catching performance car. Marketed at the lowest price ever offered for a Shelby and promoted as an exciting highway GT touring car, its sales easily topped 3,000 units.

If compromises are to be won or lost, Carroll Shelby certainly won this one. He may have had doubts at the time, but the

1967 Shelby Production Figures

GT-350 1,175 units
GT-500 2,048 units
Total 3,225 units

There was one GT-500 prototype hardtop, "Little Red," with a twin Paxton supercharged 427ci engine, built for Fred Goodell, a Ford employee who became Shelby American chief engineer. This car was eventually destroyed by Ford to avoid product liability problems. There was also one prototype 1967 GT-500 convertible that eventually became the prototype for the 1968 Shelby convertible. Evidence indicates this car still exists.

Source: 1987 *Shelby American World Registry*.

1967 SHELBY G.T. 350/500
The Road Cars

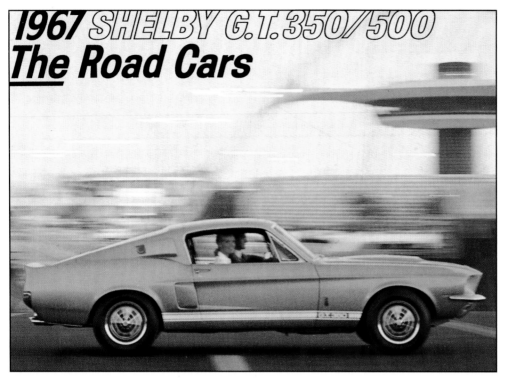

Original showroom brochure for 1967 Shelby. The six-page Shelby dealer showroom brochure targeted the affluent with lifestyle photos of a GT-350 cruising past the Los Angeles International Airport, a GT-500 in a rural, romantic setting with horseback riders, a racetrack setting, and attractive women throughout. Amidst all that, the ad copy highlighted the low price of the car compared to other domestic and imported GT models.

This fresh-looking Brittany Blue GT-500 has 15in ten-spoke wheels and center-mounted high beams, but no Le Mans stripes. The rollbar and inertia reel shoulder harnesses are plainly visible in the uncommon white interior (most were black or Parchment). The rear quarter-panel and C-pillar air scoops strongly suggest Ford's world-class GT-40 race car.

Ford's Police Interceptor 428ci engine puts the squeeze on the GT-500 engine compartment. The twin Holley 650cfm carburetors atop the aluminum medium-rise intake manifold were actuated by a dual-quad progressive linkage with vacuum secondaries. Early cars had no lettering on their aluminum oval air cleaners, but this later version has Cobra above the forward carburetor.

concept shift Ford dictated to make the Shelby more luxurious did not substantially alter the nature of the car. The small- and big-block cars were genuine muscle cars, with responsive handling, quick steering, serious brakes, and a grand heritage. At this stage of the game, the marque was rolling.

Shelby American designed unique GT-350 and GT-500 front fender emblems for 1967, and continued the use of lower body-panel stripes and model designation lettering.

SHELBY AMERICAN, INC.
6501 W. IMPERIAL HIGHWAY
LOS ANGELES, CALIFORNIA

1967
SHELBY
G.T.350/500
OWNERS MANUAL

For the 1967 Shelby GT-350 and GT-500, Shelby American, Inc., created a special cover and two ten-page Shelby-specific sections in its adaption of the standard 1967 Mustang owners manual.

The headlight housing/fender extension was incorporated into the fiberglass nose and grille surround for 1967. Many cars with outboard high-beam lights, like those on this GT-500, had a letter Z stamped in front of the serial number on the underhood VIN plate. A standard hood latch was used in conjunction with twin securing pins.

All 1967 Shelbys received the Mustang Deluxe interior, with special upholstery and molded seatbacks, fold-down rear seats, door panels with brushed-aluminum insets and molded armrests, brushed-aluminum dash trim, and aluminum trim pieces in the lower door area. Both GT-350s and GT-500s also featured the rollbar and integral inertia reel shoulder harnesses, an oil-pressure and ammeter gauge cluster under the center dash, a 1967-only steering wheel, a Shelby insignia (identical to the grille ornament) on the aluminum dash panel above the glovebox, and Shelby American logo inserts on the sill plates.

This rare white interior shows a clean example of the model-designated center horn button on the 1967 steering wheel, air conditioning ducts (also uncommon on 1967 Shelbys), the in-dash 8000rpm tachometer, and Deluxe Mustang aluminum dash trim.

Road Test:1967 Shelby GT-350 and GT-500

Acceleration, GT-350
0-30mph	2.8sec
0-40mph	4.1sec
0-50mph	5.6sec
0-60mph	7.1sec
0-70mph	9.0sec
0-80mph	11.8sec
0-90mph	15.0sec
0-100mph	19.3sec
Standing quarter-mile	91mph in 15.3sec
Top speed, observed	129mph (average, two-way run)

Acceleration, GT-500
0-30mph	2.8sec
0-40mph	4.0sec
0-50mph	4.9sec
0-60mph	6.7sec
0-70mph	8.1sec
0-80mph	11.8sec
0-90mph	15.0sec
0-100mph	16.9sec
Standing quarter-mile	92mph in 14.3sec
Top speed, observed	132mph (average, two-way run)

Engine
Type	V-8, iron block, water-cooled
Head	Cast-iron, removable
Valves	Pushrod/rocker-actuated ohv

GT-350
Max. bhp	306 at 6000rpm
Max. torque	329lb-ft at 4200rpm
Bore	4.005in
Stroke	2.87in
Displacement	289ci; 4727cc
Compression ratio	10.5:1
Induction system	Single Holley four-barrel, 750cfm
Exhaust system	Standard, dual
Electrical system	12-volt, distributor ignition
Fuel consumption	Test, 13mpg; average, 15mpg

GT-500
Max. bhp	355 at 5400rpm
Max. torque	420lb-ft at 3200rpm
Bore	4.13in
Stroke	3.984in
Displacement	428ci; 7015cc
Compression ratio	10.5:1
Induction system	Dual Holley four-barrel, 600cfm
Exhaust system	Standard, dual
Electrical system	12-volt, distributor ignition
Fuel consumption	Test, 9.4mpg; average, 11mpg

Chassis
Frame	Unit, welded
Body	Steel and fiberglass
Front suspension	Unequal arms, coil springs, adjustable tube shocks, anti-sway bar
Rear suspension	Live axle, multi-leaf springs, tube shocks
Tire type and size	Goodyear E70-15

Weights and Measures
Wheelbase	108.0in
Front track	58.0in
Rear track	58.0in
Overall height	51.6in
Overall width	70.9in
Overall length	186.6in
Ground clearance	6.5in
Crankcase	6qt
Cooling system	20qt
Gas tank	18gal
Curb weight, GT-350	2,723lb
Test weight, GT-350	3,048lb
Curb weight, GT-500	3,286lb
Test weight, GT-500	3,576lb

Clutch
Type	Single disc, dry
Diameter	10.5in
Actuation	Mechanical

Transmission
Type	Four-speed, full synchromesh

Ratios
First	2.32:1
Second	1.69:1
Third	1.29:1
Fourth	1.00:1

Brakes
Front	11.3in Kelsey-Hayes discs
Rear	10x3 drums

Differential
GT-350 ratio	3.89:1
GT-500 ratio	3.25:1
Drive axles (type)	Enclosed, semi-floating

Steering
Type	Recirculating ball
Turns, lock to lock	3.5
Turning circle	37ft

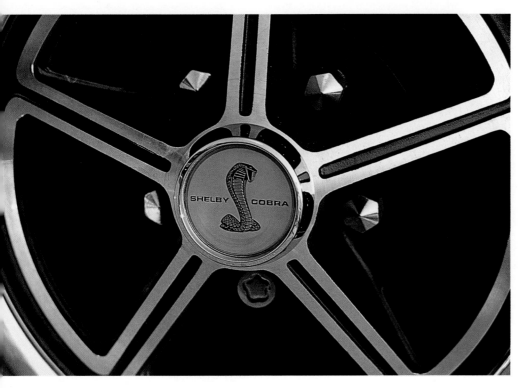

The Kelsey-Hayes 15x7 MagStar wheel was a Shelby option for 1967 only. Chromed steel rims surround aluminum center sections and Cobra logo center caps.

It is rare to find original air conditioning on the GT-350 small-block Hi-Po engine. Note the finely detailed power steering pump, date-correct fan belt, and numerous other concours touches.

"How Much Does It Cost?"

Item	Retail List
GT-350	$3,995.00
GT-500	4,195.00
Power disc brakes	64.77
Power steering	84.47
Shoulder harness	50.76
Select-O-Matic transmission	50.00
Air conditioner, Selectaire	356.09
Exhaust emission control system	45.44
Closed crankcase emission system	5.19
Fold-down rear seat	64.77
Deluxe (Shelby) wheels	185.00
Rally stripe	34.95
Paxton supercharger for GT-350	549.00

Source: *Sports Car Graphic*, March 1967.

1968 Shelby GT-350, GT-500, and GT-500KR

The Royal Treatment, and a King of the Road

The 1968 Shelby Cobra took styling to an even wilder realm than its facelifted counterpart of the previous year. From the more massive grille opening with its inset rectangular foglights to the broad, chrome-trimmed taillights, from the luxurious console-equipped interior to the highly visible convertible rollbar, the 1968 GT-350s and GT-500s radiated aggressiveness with a touch of elegance. Whereas the 1967 and 1968 Mustangs were nearly identical, the Shelbys of those years were wholly dissimilar.

At the onset of 1968 production, the two most outstanding changes were the introduction of the convertible model and the shift of production from California to Ionia, Michigan. The convertible actually had been discussed for the 1967 line, and VIN prefixes with a C in the sixth position (instead of the F for Fastback) had been outlined in FoMoCo correspondence. But it was not until the 1968 model year that a customer could obtain an open-air Shelby.

In comparing Shelby sales figures for 1967 and 1968, the increase of 1,225 vehicles coincides remarkably with the total of 1,124 convertibles produced in 1968. The distinctive design of their roll-bars certainly added to the convertibles' appeal, and Ford's promotional efforts obviously paid off.

A number of factors led to the shift of final assembly from Shelby American's huge shop near the Los Angeles International Airport to the A. O. Smith Company in Ionia, but the main factor seems to have been Ford's desire to have it that way. Quality control problems with fiberglass body pieces were solved by shifting to a Ford-found source nearer Detroit; Shelby American's plant lease would soon expire in Los Angeles; production numbers (over 3,200 in 1967 and what would become 4,450 in 1968) required a sizable capacity and a proximity to parts; and Ford's Metuchen, New Jersey, plant had become, more than San Jose and Dearborn, the assembly line most easily sourced for the Shelbys-to-be.

In order to continue their approach to expanding consumer acceptance of the Shelby, Ford offered multiple color options. The front-end design changed for 1968, with a more pronounced and rounded grille opening, inset driving lights, and scoops further forward on the hood. Instead of Klik pins, Dzus fasteners helped secure the hood and, again, the stock Mustang front bumper was used. In 1968, Shelby provided GT-350 Fastbacks to Hertz Rent-A-Car, though much fewer than in 1966, and without exterior modifications to identify the cars as Hertz models.

The rear treatments seemed to change only slightly from 1967 to 1968, but actually were substantially different. The argent panel is a fiberglass section to which 1965 Thunderbird three-bulb taillights with sequential turn indicators and a Shelby pop-open gas cap were attached. The entire tail panel then was affixed to the existing taillight panel with screws and sealer. Note the rear quarter-panel reflector assembly required for added safety on all 1968 models.

This evolution of Shelby manufacturing required a change in the company structure as well. Shelby American, Inc., remained a corporate entity, but its operations were split into three companies. Shelby Automotive, Inc., in Livonia, Michigan, coordinated the manufacture and sale of production cars; the Shelby Parts Company, in Torrance, California (which eventually moved to the Detroit area and became Shelby Autosports) handled the manufacture, purchase, and sale of Shelby aftermarket parts and accessories; and the Shelby Racing Company, in Torrance, continued and expanded racing activities.

King of the Road

Several changes in Ford's engine offerings affected the 1968 Shelby. The discontinuation of the stalwart 271hp 289ci Hi-Po (which Shelby had coaxed to the 306hp level) meant that GT-350s received a four-barrel 302ci engine. The engineers had hoped to start the year with a cast-aluminum intake manifold, but encountered trouble in passing emissions tests. The early cars received cast-iron manifolds; they were later recalled to be refitted, though many owners neglected to take part in the swap program. Rated at 250hp, the engine marked a performance reduction out of keeping with the Shelby image. The 428ci engines that had powered the previous year's GT-500s were continued in that line. Their high-rise aluminum intake manifolds were matched with 715cfm Holley carburetors, and were rated at 335hp. Toploader four-speed close-ratio transmissions were used with both engines, while C-4 automatics went to GT-350s and C-6 automatics were installed in big-block cars.

The most remarkable (and most easily promoted) engine change came after the model year was two-thirds gone: Ford introduced, in the highly touted 1968½ Mustang Cobra Jet GT and the Shelby

"King of the Road," a wonderfully reworked version of the 428 engine. The cars were launched into the realm of straight-line wildness. The Cobra Jet included revised 427 low-riser heads with expanded porting, stronger connecting rods and crankshaft, a dual-plane intake manifold, the 735cfm Holley four-barrel carburetor, and a Ram Air intake setup. Additionally, the Cobra Jets received heavy-duty front and rear shocks (four-speed cars got staggered rear shocks), front power disc brakes, power steering, and larger-capacity rear drum brakes.

It is said that the name "King of the Road" (which led to the GT-500KR designation for the late 1968 big-block Shelbys) was slated for a General Motors product. Ford got wind of the rumor, and swiped the name outright.

Oddly, Ford elected to go low-key on promoting the increased power of the Cobra Jet. Perhaps to escape the wrath of the safety-minded public and the insurance industry, the company downscaled the Cobra Jet engine horsepower rating by about twenty percent. The claim of 335hp simply wasn't correct.

The true tip-off to the nature of the 1968 Shelby could be found in the Deluxe

In 1968, for the first time, a Shelby convertible model was offered, and, for the second year, Ford promoted a premium image with the Mustang Deluxe interior in all Shelbys. The 1968 luxury interior had been redesigned to incorporate woodgrain panels. All Shelbys received a center console with oil-pressure and ammeter gauges. The Paxton supercharger was available for GT-350s and, with this installation, a fuel-pressure gauge would be mounted below the oil-pressure gauge (left side), and a manifold-boost gauge below the ammeter. This four-speed GT-350 features an optional eight-track tape player.

Cobra GT-350 and GT-500KR Special Features

- Two engine choices: GT 350, 250hp 302ci V-8; GT 500KR, 335hp 428ci V-8.
- High-velocity, high-volume Cobra intake manifold.
- Advanced design cathedral float four-barrel carburetor.
- Dual exhausts.
- Low-restriction custom paper-element diecast-aluminum air cleaner.
- Diecast-aluminum Cobra rocker covers, chromed filler cap, dipstick.
- High-rate front coil spring.
- High-capacity heavy-duty adjustable shock absorbers, front and rear.
- .94in-diameter front stabilizer bar.
- Crisp 16.0:1 steering ratio with power assist.
- Heavy-duty four-leaf rear springs.
- Anti-windup rear spring dampers for sure acceleration.
- Heavy-duty rear axle.
- Power-assisted floating caliper front disc brakes.
- Heavy-duty rear drum brakes.
- Four-ply polyglass Goodyear high-performance tires.
- 6in rim width 15in safety wheels.
- Inertia-reel shoulder harnesses and seat belts for front seat passengers (seat belts in rear).
- Integral overhead safety bar in all models.
- Safety-sequence wide taillights.
- Front marker lights.
- Rear quarter reflectors.
- Rectangular foglights.
- Dual master brake cylinder with proportioning valve and low pressure warning light.
- Collapsible steering column and safety padded center steering wheel.
- Fully unitized chassis and body.

Styling Appointments

Exterior: Precision-molded custom fiberglass hood and front assembly incorporates dual air intake scoops, functional louvered extractors. Custom self-retained push-and-turn hood locks. Rectangular foglights mounted in grille opening. Le Mans-type air extractors on rear quarters of Fastback roof. Brake air scoops set in lower quarters. Precision-molded custom fiberglass trunk deck lid with integral air spoiler. GT stripe on lower rocker panels.

Interior: Deluxe all-vinyl interior with bucket seats, full-loop pile carpeting, matching custom-styled console with padded armrest-glovebox, walnut-grained appliques on instrument panel and door panels. Full instrumentation; 8000rpm tachometer; 140mph speedometer; oil-pressure, ammeter, water temperature, and fuel gauges; electric clock. Optional folding rear seat with retractable safety luggage retaining bar (Fastback only), tie-down loops on safety bar (convertible only).

Source: Full-page advertisement for Shelby Automotive, Inc., in *Car Life*, June 1968.

In 1968, four-speed GT-350s, with their 302-4V engines, were required to run anti-smog equipment (like all GT-500s), while GT-350s with automatic transmissions ran a simpler crank-case ventilation system. All 1968 GT-350 and GT-500 Shelbys used the Cobra-lettered oval air cleaner and finned aluminum valve covers. The later GT-500KRs used Ram Air induction.

1968 Shelby Color Chart

Like the Mustang (and unlike any previous Shelby), the 1968 Shelby had a Ford warranty/data plate riveted adjacent to the driver's door latch. Colors were noted by a letter code. Interior color codes also were noted on the data plate; 1968 Shelbys offered 6A or 6AA for black vinyl, and 6F or 6FA for Medium Saddle vinyl. Both were available with any exterior color, as were black or white convertible tops. The GT side stripe was blue on a white exterior, and white on all others.

Color Code	Color Name	DuPont Number	Ditzler Number
A	Raven Black	88	9300
D	Acapulco Blue	4857	13357
I	Lime Gold	4790	43576
M	Wimbledon White	4480	8378
R	Highland Green	4869	43644
T	Candyapple Red	4737	71528
W	Fleet Yellow		
X	Dark Blue Metallic		
Y	Gold Metallic	4874	22833

1968 Shelby Production

GT-350 Fastbacks	1,253
GT-350 Convertibles	404
GT-500 Fastbacks	1,140
GT-500 Convertibles	402
GT-500KR Fastbacks	933
GT-500KR Convertibles	318
Total:	4,450

Source: 1978 *Shelby American World Registry*.

The lifestyle image building continued from 1967, and Shelby convertible rollbars even had D-rings for surfboard attachment. This GT-350 has the Marchal 656/322 foglamps that were used until sometime in April 1968. Later cars received Lucas FT8 foglamps and, in October of that year, all Marchal-equipped cars were re-called for a Lucas swap. Obviously, not all owners chose to return to the dealers. Shelby American franchised dealers numbered 111 for the 1968 model year, with nine of those located in Canada.

Cobra Jet 428 Engine Specifications

Horsepower	335 at 5600	Exhaust manifold	New header
Torque	440 at 3400	Carburetor	735cfm 4-V
Displacement	428ci	Tappet - Cam	Hydraulic
Bore	4.13in	Rocker arm	1.73:1
Stroke	3.98in	Oil pan	Conventional
Compression ratio	10.7:1	Camshaft lift	.481in intake
Cylinder heads and valves	Large intake port with 2.06in intake valve, 1.625in exhaust valve		.490in exhaust
		Camshaft duration	290deg
Intake manifold	Large iron version of aluminum manifold		

Source: Full-page advertisement for Shelby Automotive, Inc., *Car Life*, June 1968.

Mustang interior: its center console with the Cobra-embossed padded armrest and mini glovebox. Woodgrain appliques appeared on the inner door panels and dash area, but, fortunately, the oil-pressure and ammeter gauges remained, as well as the 8000rpm tachometer.

Beneath those luxury touches could be found the progressive-rate suspension used in 1967, a less-harsh ride for smoother road travel. Power brakes, power steering, shoulder harnesses, and the Fastback fold-down rear seat were mandatory options, and the Tilt-Away steering wheel was also available.

Exterior trim changed slightly in transition from 1967. The nose section was reshaped, and hoods received a wider split scoop closer to the nose, twist-type latches, and two rows of louvers near the cowl, which Shelby referred to as air extractor vents. The small rectangular front fender emblems were replaced by sculpted Cobra emblems. For a similar yet flashier look, the 1967 Cougar taillights of the 1967 Shelbys gave way to 1965 Thunderbird units with a more substantial chrome frame and five vertical chrome "teeth." The rear turn signals had sequential blinkers (except in California). These taillights would carry over to the 1969 and 1970 Shelbys as well.

As on the 1968 Mustangs, the front and rear fenders had safety reflectors near the bumper tips; the appearance of the rear reflector changed slightly during the model year. Once again, a steel 15x6 wheel was standard equipment, with a generic Ford wheelcover and Shelby logo center ornament. The Shelby cast-aluminum 15x7 ten-spoke wheels introduced in 1967 were optional for 1968.

New for 1968 were the rectangular rear fender reflectors, the 1965 Thunderbird taillights, a pop-open fuel filler cap with a Shelby Cobra center emblem, and a fresh look for Shelby exhaust tips.

The 428ci engines in GT-500s (and later GT-500KRs) were required to have anti-smog systems—hence, the blue plumbing. Unlike the previous year's big-block cars, the 1968 GT-500s were fitted with only one four-barrel carburetor, a 715cfm Holley. This fine restoration includes the Cobra Le Mans valve covers and all the smaller details needed for factory originality.

In addition to the Deluxe Mustang door panels, woodgrain dash, door panel, steering wheel appliqué, and Deluxe upholstery, Shelbys were fitted with a Cobra logo-embossed center console, a Shelby Cobra emblem at the center of the steering wheel, a GT-350 or GT-500 emblem on the dash panel above the glove compartment, and a rollbar MIG welded to the floor pan. This saddle color interior also features in-dash air conditioning.

The exterior styling of the Mustang Fastback had evolved modestly from 1965 to 1968 but, as this Candyapple Red GT-500 demonstrates, the Shelby touch dramatically upgraded the effect. The expanded grille, forward hood scoop openings, rear-quarter and C-pillar scoops, and upswept deck lid were, by themselves, minor changes. The car's tasteful statement of power contributed to the sales of over 4,400 1968 Shelby Cobras.

At the beginning of the model year, Marchal 656/322 foglights were mounted in the lower outboard corners of the grille. These were highly rated French lamps that had been used on several European cars, including several versions of Ferraris. During the production year, due to fluctuations in international currency values, the Marchal lamps became markedly more expensive for Shelby.

Because of both price and their cleaner appearance, Lucas FT8 "Square Eight" foglamps were chosen to replace the Marchals. According to Paul M. Newitt's excellent *California Special Recognition Guide and Owner's Manual*, the Lucas lights, after April 26, 1968, were installed by A. O. Smith Company on all new Shelbys and Mustang California Specials. Later, in October 1968, California ruled that the Marchals were too bright to be used safely on the highway. In response, Shelby issued a recall for the retrofit of Lucas lights for early 1968 Shelbys.

White Le Mans stripes on a Gold Metallic exterior help highlight the extended nose area and aggressive hood scoops of a 1968 Shelby. Previous year's Klik pin hood fasteners were deleted in favor of Dzus fasteners on 1968 models, and the Lucas FT8, or "square eight," foglamps replaced the Marchal units in late April 1968.

The Cobra name came into expanded usage with the decision to call the 1968 cars the Shelby Cobra. In a campaign to tie the product to the AC Cobra roadsters' rocket-like reputation, Ford's specifications sheets and most of that year's advertising stressed the term "Cobra GT." This GT-500 front fender detail shows the elaborate and elegant Cobra emblem designed for 1968 GT-350s and GT-500s. Later "King of the Road" models would get a modified version of the emblem.

In mid-April of the 1968 production year, Ford introduced the new 428ci Cobra Jet engine in the 1968½ Mustang GT. With beefed-up front shock towers, staggered rear shocks, and sturdier internal engine components, the cars seemed intended for straight-line performance. At that point, the GT-500KR replaced the GT-500, and all subsequent big-block Shelbys, through the 1970 model year, were powered by the Cobra Jet engine. The initials KR stood for King of the Road, a fitting title but, as legend has it, a name swiped from a pending General Motors project. This Candyapple Red Fastback displays the new GT-500KR side stripe and the updated front fender emblem.

The powerful lines of the twin hood scoops and Shelby lettering on the nose section proclaim the presence of power.

Not often seen on 1968 Shelbys is the subtle but elegant Highland Green exterior color. This car also has the cast-aluminum ten-spoke wheels and Tilt-Away steering wheel. The GT-500KR also received dual-quad exhaust outlet tips and a unique Cobra Jet inset emblem for its pop-open fuel filler caps.

Next page
"Try the complete surprise. . . ." Lifestyle is for sale when a new car is photographed next to a private jet or zipping along a beach just yards away from the crashing surf. Pleasure, comfort, styling, and safety are being promoted: "a richly fitted console;" "full instrumentation;" "high-intensity fog lights and other safety items;" "deep bucket seats;" "strictly limited editions designed by Carroll Shelby. . . ." Is this what the former chicken farmer-turned road racer really had in mind?

The KR-model Shelbys' fender emblem combined the sculpted cobra, the words Cobra Jet, and the numerals 428.

Try the <u>complete</u> surprise...
Carroll Shelby's COBRA GT

Carroll Shelby reasons that a *true* GT needs *everything* for high performance pleasure, comfort and safety engineered right in, not just offered as afterthought options. That's why his Cobra GT is a *complete* surprise to those who see it and drive it for the first time. □ Surprise number one is style. Subtle changes in grille, hood, sides, rear deck add a fresh, exclusive look. Interior luxury follows through with deep-bucket seats, walnut-grain appliques, front seat center console-armrest, courtesy lights, full instrumentation. □ Naturally, you expect performance ... but the GT 500's Shelby-ized 428 cubic inch V-8 rewrites the performance charts with surprising smoothness. A 302 V-8 is Shelby-prepared for the GT 350. Special wide-path tires, 16-to-1 power steering, modified suspension and adjustable super-duty shocks deliver firm control but with enough velvet to make an all-day trip a pleasure. □ Safety features are engineered-in, too. These include an overhead safety bar and inertia-reel shoulder harnesses, impact-absorbing steering wheel, dual braking system. □ By engineering his other surprises into the great-to-start-with Mustang, Carroll Shelby's biggest surprise is the small price. □ Your Shelby dealer will prove just how big *that* surprise can be.

Shelby COBRA GT 350/500   POWER BY Ford

77

Carroll Shelby's COBRA GT
...for the man who wants everything in one car

Distinctive styling, superb performance, reassuring safety—you can have all these at an attractively low price. ☐ Both the custom-styled Cobra GT convertible and the 2+2 fastback are strictly limited editions designed by Carroll Shelby (no meeting yourself around every corner). ☐ Exterior styling features are distinctive *and* functional — hood scoops for carburetor air, fastback louvers as air extractors. Even sequential tail lights. ☐ Interiors are luxurious. They gleam with unique simulated wood grain on instrument panel, steering wheel and door trim. There's a richly fitted console. ☐ These *road* car features were designed by *racing* car builders for you: new 302 Ford V-8 (GT 350) or 428 Ford V-8 (GT 500); disc front brakes; competition-based suspension; heavy-duty driveline and rear axle; custom hi-performance 130 MPH rated nylon tires; wide-rim wheels; full instrumentation with an 8,000 RPM tachometer; 4-speed transmission (a close-coupled automatic is a low-cost option). ☐ Cobra's safety features are built-in. These include front seat shoulder harnesses, high intensity fog lights and other safety items. Integral overhead bar is standard in both models. ☐ Carroll Shelby engineered all these features into the Mustang, winner of two Trans-Am road racing championships. ☐ Result: '68 Cobras that rival Europe's finest limited production cars— but sell for thousands of dollars less. ☐ Try "everything" at your Shelby Cobra dealer.

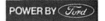

Shelby COBRA GT 350/500   POWER BY Ford

If Ford wanted the ultimate cruising GT, the 500KR convertible, with its luxury interior, air conditioning, tinted glass, AM/FM stereo, and close to 400hp, certainly filled the bill. Only 318 were produced during the period between the introduction of the Cobra Jet package and the end of the 1968 model year.

In late April 1968, due to owner complaints and state regulations, the Marchal 656/322 grille-mounted foglamps were replaced by these Lucas FT8 units, which required a custom-fabricated mounting bracket.

The two-piece folding glass rear window of this Acapulco Blue KR convertible was a $38.86 option for 1968 Mustangs. Shipping tie-down plate removal instructions for receiving dealers are on the paper affixed to the center rear valance.

The Cobra Jet engine used a Ram Air induction system, so the blue circular air cleaner and snorkel arrangement replaced the signature Cobra aluminum oval. The fiberglass chamber fitting to the underside of the hood funneled outside air directly to the air cleaner.

Overall, the 1968 Shelby represented a nod toward performance and a salute toward powerful highway cruising. Again, the public responded and, again, sales figures climbed. Still many steps above a standard Mustang, the Shelby offered a mixed message to enthusiasts. As *Motor Trend* pointed out in March 1968, "The 'establishment' has had its impact on Shelby American, and they've succumbed and resisted. Styling reflects the adoption of the 'great' philosophy, but performance and safety still are Shelby's own exclusives."

The Shelby nose consisted of the lower panel assembly, upper panel (to which the letters Shelby were affixed), and two side panels to shroud the headlights. Note the special attaching brackets that hold the Shelby grille to the forward hood bumpers and the two brackets that connect to the upper panel assembly.

With a 735cfm Holley four-barrel, low-riser heads from Ford's 427 engine, dished pistons, and strengthened connecting rods and crankshaft, the 428ci KR engine produced a nominal 335hp. Most folks knew that figure was an attempt by Ford to low-ball the power rating.

The 1969 Shelby de Mexico GT-350 was a Mexican-built Mustang hardtop with fiberglass roofline extensions and a vinyl roof. It sported 15in ten-spoke wheels and ran an upgraded 302ci engine. Courtesy Eduardo Velázquez.

Shelby de Mexico
Dust Clouds in the Neighbor's Yard.

In 1965, Mexican auto parts distributor Eduardo Velázquez bought a Hi-Po 1965 Mustang hardtop and delivered it to Hi-Performance Motors in Los Angeles for conversion to competitive status. Equipped with a race-ready 289ci engine and the complete Shelby suspension, the Mustang became a winner in Mexico. By the end of 1966, Velázquez's team had won ten of the seventeen events they had raced.

Ford Motor Company, S.A., the Mexican branch of the corporation, had begun producing Mustang hardtops. During 1966, Velázquez became a Shelby parts dealer, and the victories provided great promotion for Shelby aftermarket parts for those Mustangs. In 1967, Velázquez formed a friendship and partnership with Carroll Shelby. Their company, Shelby de Mexico, would create modified Mustangs to be marketed through Ford of Mexico dealerships.

The Shelby de Mexico models of 1967 and 1968 were powered by 289ci engines and looked nearly identical to their 1967 and 1968 stateside namesakes. Production totaled 169 units in 1967 and 203 units in 1968.

The 306 Shelbys produced in 1969 were based on 302hp-powered Mustang hardtops, but had fiberglass roofline extensions that created a Fastback look. Their front sheetmetal was near-stock Mustang, but the slightly bulged hoods were fiberglass, their deck lids had spoilers, and the taillights were the 1965 Thunderbird units used by US production 1968 and 1969 Shelbys. Several of the 1969 Shelby de Mexico GT-350s have been brought into the United States during recent years, and two have been featured in *Mustang Monthly* and other enthusiast magazines.

During those years, Shelby de Mexico campaigned Mustang race cars throughout Mexico, including two Shelby-built 1966 and 1967 Group 2 hardtops. Much advice was received from Al Dowd, Phil Remington, and Lew Spencer at Shelby American, and Carroll Shelby made a point of attending several races in Mexico. The company created two race cars in 1969 and only one in 1970. Only one of those race-specific models is known to survive.

Shelby de Mexico, during the 1971 model year, built approximately 200 Shelby Mustang GT-351s (Windsor engines) and 300 Shelby Mavericks powered by 302hp engines.

In 1967, Freddy Van Beuren won twelve races in Mexico driving one of the earliest 1967 Shelby de Mexico hardtops. Courtesy Eduardo Velázquez.

Memo Rojas drove a Shelby de Mexico race car (based on a 1969 Mustang hardtop) to a class victory at the Mexico City Race Track in 1969. Courtesy Eduardo Velázquez.

The only significant changes to the GT-500KR Deluxe interior were the additions of a wooden Cobra-logo shifter handle and a new Cobra Jet medallion on the panel above the glove compartment. This Fastback model also has optional in-dash air conditioning.

Shelby Europa
Fourteen Cars into the History Books.

Belgian road-racing veteran Claude DuBois, a Ford of Belgium employee and a Shelby dealer, campaigned 5R209, a Shelby R-Model, for Ford of Belgium throughout 1967. By 1969, he had become Shelby's direct importer for the European Common Market, and his stock had included approximately 125 Cobras and Shelbys, as well as numerous De Tomaso Mangustas and products of AC Cars.

When Ford and Shelby elected to close down the GT-350/GT-500 program in the United States, DuBois found himself in a dilemma. He would not have the volume to remain in business. In a creative move, he proposed to Carroll Shelby that he would oversee the continuing production of Shelby Mustangs in Europe. The cars would be based on 351ci 1971 Mustang convertibles, Mach 1s, and standard SportsRoofs.

While Shelby agreed to the "Shelby Europa" plan and the cars were no-nonsense performers in the same spirit of the mid-1960s versions, only fourteen cars were built before the project was halted in 1972. No factory records were kept for these cars, but thanks to owner response to SAAC queries, a handful have been located in northern Europe and New Zealand.

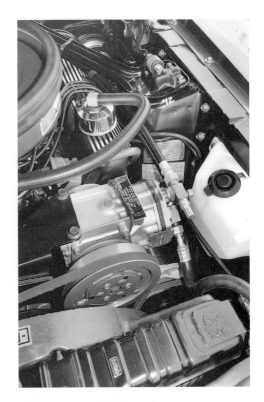

In addition to the Mustang Deluxe instrument cluster, this Shelby has the optional Tilt-Away steering wheel. Note the location of the climate controls and the left-side air conditioning register.

This Cobra Jet engine also drives an original air conditioning compressor. The shock towers of CJ cars were reinforced at their bases. The inner fender detailing of this car helps make it a concours champion.

The passenger-side dash emblem indicates a
Cobra Jet, as does the Cobra logo wooden
shifter handle.

The GT-500KR side stripe and Cobra Jet 428 fender emblem appeared on only 318 convertibles and 933 fastbacks.

When Shelby production moved from California to Michigan, Shelby American split into several entities. Shelby Automotive, Inc., named on the doorsill plate, oversaw the building and selling of the automobiles.

In 1968, a Dzus twist-type hood lock, positioned adjacent to the leading edge of the hood scoop, replaced the Klik pins of previous years.

Two different designs of rear fender reflectors were used in 1968 to comply with new highway safety regulations.

Next page
Original spec sheet: 1968 Shelby Cobra GT 350/500. Dated August 1967, this general-specification flyer helped to launch the new-for-1968 convertible model with its "overhead safety bar." Presumably, it could not be called a rollbar because of implied protection and potential liability. The sheet also lists the specs for the optional "all-new Cobra hydraulic OHV 427ci V-8." Though it never actually appeared in production, the engine was rated at 400hp at 5600rpm; 460 lb-ft of torque at 3200 rpm; with a compression ratio of 11.6:1.

The Shelby lettering on the flared fiberglass deck lid, the Cobra Jet pop-open gas cap, and the striking 1965 Thunderbird taillights provide an elegantly simple, yet strong, rear view.

marketing office

shelby automotive inc.
box 7390, north end station
detroit, michigan 48202

Dear Friend:

Thanks for your request for information about my Shelby Cobra GT cars. The enclosed material should give you a pretty complete idea of what these cars are like.

Please note that my new GT 500-KR is being marketed in addition to the GT 350 and GT 500 described in the color brochure. The GT 500-KR is powered by Ford's fantastic new Cobra Jet 428 cubic inch V-8. I've Shelby-ized it a little, for just a tweak more top-end performance, although it's pretty unbelievable as it is. (The Cobra Jet replaces the 427 engine which was proposed but not produced for '68.)

You'll find a Cobra dealer not too far from you. He'll be glad to answer your questions about prices, trade-ins, terms, delivery, options and equipment...and to give you the pleasure of trying a new Cobra GT 350, GT 500 or GT 500-KR for yourself.

Thanks again for your interest in Shelby cars.

Cordially,

Carroll Shelby
Carroll Shelby

builders of fine sports cars • Cobra GT-350 / GT-500

Original letter responding to KR information request. This letter, mailed from Shelby Automotive, Inc., in Detroit to anyone requesting information on the 1968 Shelbys, accompanied the standard literature packet. It is interesting to note the mention that the Cobra Jet engine "replaces the 427 engine which was proposed but not produced for 1968."

SHELBY COBRA GT 350/500
SPECIFICATIONS & FEATURES

All-new GT 350 and GT 500 convertibles feature integral overhead safety bar, many other performance, handling, safety and comfort features.

Get behind the wheel of a Shelby Cobra GT and you command a new motoring dimension. Carroll Shelby has worked a bit of racing car magic on the Ford Mustang. Result? The Shelby Cobra GT . . . a **true** road performer that rivals Europe's finest limited-production cars—but for thousands of dollars less. □ That's not all the news. Now you can own a Cobra GT 350 or GT 500 **convertible!** Same great features as the famed GT 350 and GT 500 fastback 2+2 coupes. □ If you love driving, you'll appreciate the pleasure of Cobra's thrilling GT performance and exclusive styling. It's a pleasure you can afford, as your Shelby Cobra dealer will gladly prove.

YOUR COBRA DEALER

ENGINE SPECIFICATIONS

GT 350

Standard: All new OHV 302 cu. in. V-8; 250 horsepower @ 4800 rpm; 310 lbs./foot of torque @ 2800 rpm; 4.0" x 3.0" bore and stroke; compression ratio 10.5:1; hydraulic valve lifters. Cobra high velocity high volume intake manifold with 4 bbl carburetor with 600 CFM flow rate.

Optional*: Cobra centrifugal supercharger, 335 horsepower @ 5200 rpm; 325 lbs./foot of torque @ 3200 rpm.†

NOTE: All Cobra GT engines include high velocity high flow intake manifolds, die-cast aluminum rocker covers, low restriction oval design diecast aluminum air cleaner, chromed filler caps, high capacity fuel pumps.

GT 500

Standard: All new Cobra OHV 428 cu. in. V-8; 360 horsepower @ 5400 rpm; 420 lbs./foot of torque @ 3200 rpm; 4.13" x 3.984" bore and stroke; compression ratio 10.5:1; hydraulic valve lifters. Cobra high velocity high volume intake manifold with advanced design, 4 bbl Holley carburetor with 600 CFM (flow rate) primaries, 715 CFM secondaries. High capacity fuel pump.

Optional*: All new Cobra hydraulic OHV 427 cu. in. V-8; 400 horsepower @ 5600 rpm; 460 lbs./foot of torque @ 3200 rpm; 4.235" x 3.788" bore and stroke; compression ratio 11.6:1; hydraulic valve lifters, advanced design cathedral float 4 bbl Holley carburetor. High capacity fuel pump.**

Buy It . . . or watch it go by

King of the Road!

Carroll Shelby has pulled the trick of the year. He's combined Ford's new *drag champion* 428 Cobra Jet engine with his *complete* road car, the Cobra GT 500. Result? Cobra GT 500-KR . . . King of the Road.

Drag champion engine? The 428 Cobra Jet grabbed Super Stock Eliminator honors at the Pomona Winternationals. It delivers 335 hp at 5400 rpm, churns up 440 lbs/ft of torque at a usable 3400. Look for 0 to 60 times that will snap your eyeballs! "Hot Rod" Magazine calls it ". . . the fastest-running Pure Stock in the history of man."

The complete Shelby Cobra GT is ready-made for the "all-there" Cobra Jet. Power is controlled by adjustable shocks, heavy-duty suspension, four-speed transmission (with automatic a low cost option), beefy driveline and torque-sensitive locking rear. All standard—along with 16-to-1 ratio power steering, high performance tires, power disc front brakes. These essentials—plus safety features, luxury interiors and limited-edition styling—are engineered-in, not just offered as options.

The game is Follow-the-Leader. The name of the game is Cobra GT 500-KR. Or play a slightly tamer game with the Cobra GT 350. But make your play at your Shelby dealer . . . today.

 Shelby COBRA GT 350/500-KR

Original dealer brochure: 1968 Shelby Cobra GT 350/500. The first piece of dealer literature regarding the 1968 Shelby Cobra GT-350/500 had a printing date of August 15, 1967. "Just for fun," it says, "Drive the Race-Proved Road Cars." It touts the Goodyear Speedway 350 tires and only seven colors: Red, Lime Gold, White, Gold Frost, Acapulco Blue, Black, and Dark Green. One photograph has Carroll Shelby posing next to a red convertible and green fastback, with an airport in the background. The fastback sports an early-design 350 fuel filler cap insert.

Original dealer promo postcard. Standard for 1968 Shelbys was the generic 15in Ford wheel cover with Shelby center cap shown on this original promotional postcard. The ten-spoke cast-aluminum wheel was optional. The models posing with the two cars are not road-racing types; obviously, the sales pitch had moved upscale during the Shelby Mustang's midlife crisis.

Just for fun . . .
DRIVE THE RACE-PROVED ROAD CARS

'68 Shelby
COBRA GT 350/500

1969-1970 Shelby - The Last Big Storm

Beauty and Power.
But the Mustangs Were Catching Up

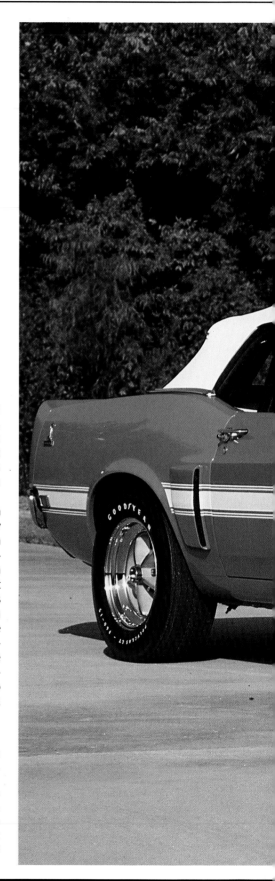

The 1969 Shelby enjoyed what many felt to be the most elegant styling of the 1969-1973 Mustang era. With the first fiberglass front fenders since the marque's inception, its unique full-width grille opening, wild NACA-scooped hood, striking rear view, and Shelby-only front bumper, the car had a significance all its own. For the third straight year, its styling made it stand apart from the standard Mustang—but maybe not far enough.

Introduced during the same model year as the successful Mach 1, the venerated Boss 429, and the rugged Boss 302, the 1969 Shelby GT-350s and GT-500s found their toughest competition close to home. Equipped with the Mustang's new Windsor block 351-4V in the GT-350s, and the 428ci Cobra Jet engines introduced to Mustang GTs and Shelby GT-500s late in the 1968 model year, the newest Shelbys had to compete with three new Mustang performance Fastback models—now called SportsRoofs—in action as well as appearance.

The Shelby was described in the February 1969 *Sports Car Graphic* as, "No longer a Mustang look-alike." But under the skin, they were more similar to Mustangs than their predecessors, and that caused consternation in the automotive media. Brock Yates, then senior editor at

Car and Driver, called it "a garter snake in Cobra skin." Oddly, three sentences later, he wrote, "I personally can't think of an automobile that makes a statement about performance in sheet metal and fiberglass any better than the current edition of the GT-350."

Once again, base vehicle production was shifted, this time from Metuchen, New Jersey, where the 1968 Shelbys had begun their existence, to Ford's Dearborn assembly plant. From there, the knockdown models went to Shelby Automotive's plant in Ionia, Michigan. The SportsRoof was based on a Mach 1 (data code 63C), which came with its own Deluxe interior, and the convertibles began as data code 76B Deluxe interior models. Dozens of unique components were added in the Shelby Automotive second stage, and the changes to the Shelby exteriors read somewhat like a map of scoops and badges.

Because the Ford stylists assigned to the 1969 Shelby project were able to replace the Mustang front fenders with custom fiberglass pieces, they enjoyed more latitude in redesigning the final Shelby. Even the front bumper was unique to the GT-350/500 models. This Grabber Blue convertible gives a clear view of the trademark Shelby rear-quarter scoops that fed cool air to the inner fenderwell and rear brakes.

The 1969 and 1970 Shelbys were identical except for the chin spoiler, twin black hood stripes, VIN codes, and additional emissions equipment on the later models. The Grabber Orange on this 1970 GT-350 convertible was also available on Mustangs in 1970. Styled wheels, chromed steel rims with cast-aluminum centers, were standard on all 1969 and 1970 models, and Shelby Automotive offered no optional wheel.

The annual SAAC conventions provide members the opportunities to drive their vintage performance vehicles on racetracks, coast to coast. This unmodified 1969 GT-350 SportsRoof is doing what comes naturally at the 1989 Pocono SAAC event.

This Grabber Green 1970 GT-500 convertible displays the updated 428 Cobra Jet emblem on its upper rear front fender. The roll bars for the 1969-1970 Shelbys were not as substantial as the 1967-1968 versions, nor were they MIG-welded to the floor pan as they had been. Only the SportsRoof models used inertia reel front seat safety harnesses. The reflective full-length mid-bodyside tape stripes, in blue, gold, white, and black, keyed off the exterior colors.

One is first drawn to the grille, with its inset chromed rectangle and offset Cobra insignia. The extended, sculptured hood boasts three air inlet scoops, two relief vents just forward of the firewall, and chromed twist-type latches. The fiberglass front fenders have scoops just aft of the grille and ahead of the wheel openings. They may or may not be effective in cooling the front disc brakes, but the quarter-panel scoops ahead of the rear wheel openings are specifically ducted to route air to the

rear drums. The convertible quarter-panel scoops are more oblong and are positioned lower than the SportsRoof versions so their ducting can clear the convertible top mechanism. There was no roof-mounted air scoop for 1969.

The trademark Shelby lower body panel stripe, in a change mirrored by the new Mach 1, was moved upward to draw the eye from the headlight rearward, ending at the rear bumper. The reflective tape stripes came in white, gold, blue, and black to complement the cars' exterior colors. There was only one style of 1969-1970 wheel: a hefty-looking five-spoke aluminum center in a chrome steel rim with a Cobra logo center cap.

At the rear of the car, 1965 Thunderbird taillight reflector housings, lenses, and chrome bezels filled a fiberglass taillight panel. The gas filler inlet was hidden behind the hinged license frame, so no special cap was needed. Just below the

license frame, a custom aluminum exhaust outlet handled the dual exhausts. This location led to a problem several months into production: The GT-500 models, after decelerating from highway speed, could backfire and ignite fuel vapors collected in a "dead air" spot above the filler cap. This almost always occurred to cars that had had the distributor timing advanced and either the fuel mixture or carburetor jets changed. The fires would damage the fiberglass tailpanel and deck lid.

A proper recall was put in motion, and owners of record were notified of the fire hazard by a September 18, 1969, letter from Ford's National Service Office. A September 16 letter to Shelby dealers provided detailed instructions on carrying out the recall, replacing the vent-type gas filler cap and installing a vent tube to direct fumes under the car to a framerail area.

Finally, the fiberglass deck lid again matched custom fender extensions, and a

The Factory Had It Rough

The 1969 Shelbys were built under District Special Order (DSO) codes allocated to Ford's Home Office Reserve. Therefore, every 1969 Shelby door data plate DSO code begins with 84. It is known that, at times, several vehicles would be ordered under a single six-digit DSO number. These knockdown models, or Base Vehicle Shells, could be delivered for conversion and sale only to dealer 84-999, the Shelby Automotive Company. The final six digits of their VIN codes would begin with 48 (with one or two exceptions on the earliest prototypes).

Creating the 1969 Mustangs to be shipped to Shelby Automotive's Ionia, Michigan, plant was directed by a Special Competitive Vehicle Product Letter dated July 19, 1968, and issued August 15, 1968. The vehicle release and special equipment parts list indicated that four separate situations be recognized:

Parts List 9393-400 provided guidelines for modifying a Mach 1 to Shelby specifications. Everything from omitting the production steps of drilling sheet metal holes for Mach 1 trim to installing a Cougar console (C9WB-65045A06-N1A) was included.

Parts List 9393-450 upgraded a base Mustang convertible to Shelby specs. From the addition of the GT Equipment Group and Mach 1 Sound Package to the deletion of interior rear-quarter trim (where the rollbar would be installed), the steps were detailed. Preparing the front ends for Shelby's unique fiberglass pieces and custom grille/bumper assembly required the systematic deletion from the Mustang process of eighty-four separate components. At least sixty-four additional deletions were needed to complete the task.

Parts list 9393-350 directed the creation of the factory input to the GT-350 package. Because the fastbacks began as Mach 1s and the convertibles as base (no option) convertibles, certain items such as the Heavy Duty (or GT) suspension and Deluxe Interior were already standard for a Mach 1. Only the Shelby convertibles received specific instructions to add those two items. The Mustang shocks were replaced with Gabriel Adjustables (C9ZX-18045-B, front; C9ZX-18080-C, rear), the exhaust system was readied for the Shelby rear exhaust outlets, and 0.95in stabilizer bars replaced 0.85in units. Even details such as the inclusion of Cougar-type gearshift knobs (C8WA-7213-C) for four-speed cars and the addition of a C4DB-16A238-A radiator support-to-hood rubber seal were listed.

Parts list 9393-500 directed the factory input to the GT-500 package. Here, the convertibles got high-back bucket seats with knitted vinyl trim, the Deluxe Interior Decor Group, the tachometer and trip odometer for automatic transmission cars, and power tops with glass backlights. The Cougar-style 428-4V air cleaner for Ram Air (C9ZF-9600-D) was slated to replace the C9ZF-9600-E Mustang unit; likewise, a C7ZF-9601-A air cleaner element and C7ZF-9661-A cover assembly were noted. Part number C9ZX-5556-A two-stage rear springs replaced those slated for Mach 1s (C9ZA-5556-G) and convertibles (C9ZA-5556-E). Dozens of other changes were made before the Base Vehicle Shells left Ford's Dearborn Assembly Plant.

The updated Shelby rear end received fresh styling through the use of fiberglass rear-fender end caps and a deck-lid treatment similar to the 1967-1968 models. The fiberglass taillight panel incorporated a gas filler cap behind the license plate frame, the 1965 Thunderbird taillights adapted for 1968 Shelbys were carried over to 1969-1970, and a unique aluminum center exhaust outlet was mounted just under the rear bumper.

chrome-trimmed black expanded aluminum section was inset vertically into both the deck lid and extensions. Similar aluminum pieces also were inset into the two most forward hood scoops and the rear quarter-panel scoops.

The End of the Road

This is not a mystery book, so the reader knows that the 1969 model was, for all intent, the final Shelby Mustang. Carroll Shelby had seen his small manufacturing operation outgrow two facilities, generate volumes of dominating race cars, and bring unending attention to Ford and to the teams and work force of Shelby American. He also had seen it moved away from California and closer to Ford, and had seen the initial, highly successful "Cobra-Mustang" program become twisted by the demands of the corporation and the marketplace. He had seen the muscle cars of the era begin to receive increased scrutiny from the powers of government and insur-

---

Road Test Specifications, 1969 Shelby GT-500

Options

as Tested:	Traction-Lok, fold-down rear seat, Tilt-Away steering wheel, automatic transmission, AM radio

Engine

Type	V-8, iron block, water-cooled
Head	Cast-iron, removable
Valves	Pushrod/rocker-actuated ohv
Maximum bhp	335 at 5200rpm
Maximum torque	440lb-ft at 3400rpm
Bore	4.13in
Stroke	3.98in
Displacement	428ci; 7019cc
Compression ratio	10.7:1
Induction system	Ram Air, single Holley four-barrel carburetor
Exhaust system	Standard, dual
Electrical system	12 volt, distributor ignition

Transmission

Type	Three-speed automatic with manual override

Ratios

First	2.46:1
Second	1.46:1
Third	1.00:1

Differential

Ratio	Hypoid, 3.50:1
Drive axles (type)	Enclosed, semi-floating

Steering

Type	Recirculating ball-and-nut-type gear, power-assisted
Turns, lock to lock	3.5
Turning circle	37ft

Brakes

Type	Ventilated front discs; heavy-duty drum rear, dual system, power-assisted
Disc diameter	11.3in
Drum diameter	10.0in

Chassis

Frame	Unit steel, welded
Body	Steel and fiberglass
Front suspension	Unequal A-arms, independent coil springs, anti-sway bar, heavy-duty adjustable tube shocks
Rear suspension	Hotchkiss-type, unsymmetrical, variable-rate semi-elliptical leaf springs, heavy-duty adjustable tube shocks
Tire type and size	Goodyear Super Wide-Oval F60x15

Weights and Measures

Wheelbase	108.0in
Front track	58.5in
Rear track	58.5in
Overall height	50.6in
Overall width	71.9in
Overall length	190.62in
Ground clearance	6in
Curb weight	3,850lb
Test weight	4,230lb
Crankcase	6qt
Cooling system	20qt
Gas tank	18gal

Acceleration

0-30mph	2.4sec
0-40mph	3.5sec
0-50mph	4.7sec
0-60mph	6.0sec
0-70mph	7.3sec
0-80mph	9.0sec
0-90mph	11.6sec
0-100mph	13.9sec
Standing quarter-mile	102mph in 14sec
Top speed, observed	115mph

Fuel consumption

Test	9.4mpg
Average	11-12mpg

Braking Test

Deceleration average	.73g
Fade	Encountered on seventh stop

Source: *Sports Car Graphic*, February 1969.

Ford officially renamed the Mustang Fastback the SportsRoof, and the Shelby GT-350s (like this Black Jade model) and GT-500s were based directly on the new-for-1969 Mustang Mach 1. SportsRoof Shelbys had their rear-quarter-brake cooling scoops mounted higher for 1969 and 1970, just aft of the doorhandles. Note the eye-catching Mach 1 red inserts on the front seat backs.

Next page
Inlaid into the deck spoiler and fender end caps of 1969-1970 Shelbys were sections of expanded aluminum. This Grabber Blue Sports-Roof also has optional rear window slats.

The Shelby interior for 1969 and 1970, adapted from the Mustang Mach 1 interior, included the Mach 1 woodgrain dash treatment with a Shelby emblem.

1969 Shelby Color Chart

Like the 1968 Shelby and its 1969 Mustang counterpart, the 1969 Shelby had a Ford warranty/data plate riveted adjacent to the driver's door latch. Colors were noted by a letter code. Interior color codes also were noted on the data plate; 1969 Shelbys offered 3A for black vinyl, 3W for white vinyl, and 3D for red vinyl.

Color Code	Color Name	DuPont Number	Ditzler Number
B	Royal Maroon	4864	50746
C	Black Jade	88	9300
D	Acapulco Blue	4857	13357
F	Gulfstream Aqua	4868	13329
M	Wimbledon White	4480	8378
T	Candyapple Red	4737	71528
J	Grabber Blue	5205	2230
U	Grabber Orange	5208	2232
Z	Grabber Green	5206	2231
4	Silver Jade	4975	2048
6	Pastel Gray	5053	2038
None	Grabber Yellow	5194	2214

1969 Shelby Prices

GT-350 SportsRoof	$4,434.00
GT-350 Convertible	4,753.00
GT-500 SportsRoof	4,709.00
GT-500 Convertible	5,027.00

One of the minor changes that differentiated the 1970 Shelbys from the 1969 models was a twin-stripe hood paint scheme. The stripes began at the lip just forward of the NACA ducts and ended at the aft edge behind the air extractors.

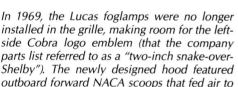

In 1969, the Lucas foglamps were no longer installed in the grille, making room for the left-side Cobra logo emblem (that the company parts list referred to as a "two-inch snake-over-Shelby"). The newly designed hood featured outboard forward NACA scoops that fed air to the engine compartment.

ance. He had seen what happens when a pet project outgrows its purpose. None of it looked good to a stubborn, independent, promo-minded, throttle-jumping, race-winning competitor.

Shelby had created race cars in 1965; only several years later, the automobiles were, to his mind, boulevard cruisers headed in a direction he did not comprehend or enjoy. He asked Ford Motor Company to bring the pact to an end.

Almost 800 1969 Shelbys remained unsold as Ford's 1970 sales season began. To prevent their instant devaluation and to ease their sale through Ford dealerships, the remaining 1969 stock was converted into 1970 models through minor changes and the major change of updating their windshield VIN plates. To remain within the law, Shelby Automotive asked the FBI to oversee the renumbering process. To update the cars, black stripes were added to the hoods, door data decals were changed, and emissions controls were brought up to 1970 standards. Lower front spoilers, similar to those on Boss 302 Mustangs, were shipped with the 1970 Shelbys to be added by dealers after the hazardous rides on the transport trucks.

Oddly, there are conflicts in the old paperwork regarding the total number of 1969-1970 Shelbys produced. The official Ford tally, based on a document from 1969, is 3,153 units. But the Shelby American Automobile Club, based on serial numbers observed, holds that as many as 3,294 were made. Either way, looking back, the numbers indicate a reasonably successful swan song sales record.

Finally, the production operation ceased. Fortunately, in intent and image, the Shelby maintained its reputation and mystique through the waning days of the era. Wonderfully, today, it all survives.

The familiar Cobra logo/Shelby emblem was positioned on the SportsRoof C-pillars.

Consoles in the 1969 and 1970 Shelbys were adapted from Mercury Cougar units.

A Cobra Jet GT-500 emblem replaces this Shelby's Mustang Mach 1 emblem on the wood-grain passenger dash area. Note the wood shifter handle, stock in-dash Mustang air conditioning vents, and Shelby gauges mounted in the console.

Taillights from the 1965 Thunderbird were used on all Shelby Mustangs after 1967. Note the expanded aluminum insert in the flared sections of the rear-fender extensions and deck lid.

Shelby Automotive installed a Cobra logo steering wheel center insert, a wood shift handle (CJ cars had cobras on the handle), and consoles from the Mercury Cougar line.

The 1969-1970 fuel filler cap is located behind the flip-down license plate bracket. The first caps were vented, and the proximity of fumes to the aluminum exhaust outlet caused fires that damaged the adjacent fiberglass panels. After eleven fires were reported between early May and mid-July, Ford issued a Special Service Letter dated July 14, 1969, instructing dealers to modify GT-500s in stock so that their gas tanks would vent into a frame rail. On July 22, an internal Product Development Letter recommended a recall of the 567 cars in the hands of individuals and the 784 cars held by dealers (1,351 total) as of July 11. In September, Ford issued a formal recall to all GT-500 owners.

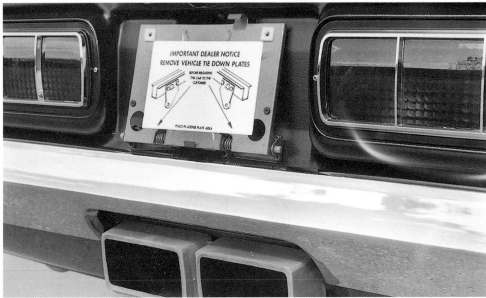

All 1969 and 1970 Shelbys used Ram Air induction. This 428ci Cobra Jet engine compartment incorporates not only the complete anti-smog system, but the correct factory quality control markings and properly dated hoses. Its 735cfm Holley carburetor and aluminum intake manifold are flanked by finned aluminum valve covers.

Previous page
This underside detail of the Ram Air hood used on all 1969 and 1970 Shelbys, regardless of engine size, shows that the outboard forward NACA scoops fed air to the engine compartment, while the center scoop led directly to the Ram Air assembly. The two rear-facing extractors near the cowl allowed heated air to escape the engine compartment.

Afterword

One of Carroll Shelby's earliest performance claims was that a Cobra roadster could go from a standstill to 100mph and back to a standstill in 12sec flat. That, of course, was almost unbelievable for any car. But books should not screech to a halt.

Let's jump away from the year-by-year production, sales, and competition of the 1960s, and close out this history with an overview of what we now observe.

These days, we seem to be witnessing a cross between a benevolent personality cult and a de-centralized marketing empire. Just as Florida tourist concessionaires know that any ashtray, T-shirt, lamp, or housing development will sell faster if a palm tree is attached to it, the auto paraphernalia vendors of the world know the effect of the name Shelby. Of course, the various Shelby trademarks and the use of the name are vigorously policed by an experienced staff. But the fact cannot be disputed: The name carries a cachet of power, class, adventure, and money.

Carroll Shelby tours the SAAC-16 popular vote car show at Charlotte Motor Speedway with Lee Morse of Ford Special Vehicle Operations (a Cobra roadster owner) and Howard Pardee, an R-Model owner and member of the SAAC.

Recent years have seen an escalation in values for the cars and comparisons to the great European builders. Legends grow under their own steam. All individuals can do is witness and contribute, recognize and perpetuate. The history of the Shelby evolves: More production details will be discovered, more people will become fascinated by the marque, and attention and respect will grow with time. It all stems from the personality, instinct, gumption, inventions, and wisdom of one man.

Carroll Shelby went to work for Chrysler in the early 1980s. When pressed by an earnest fan for reasons behind his apparent defection, Shelby explained his move succinctly: Lee Iacocca was the main individual at Ford who got behind the 289 Cobra concept. Iacocca, then the Ford Division Sales Manager, went out on a professional limb to front money and support so that Shelby American could become a reality.

There came a time when both Chrysler and Iacocca were in trouble. Carroll Shelby offered his assistance. And that's all there was to it. The man would not forget the origins of the phenomenon. He would not let a brand loyalty displace a personal loyalty.

The man believed in what could be done, stuck by his guns, built cars of character, proved what could be done,

and, when the project sidetracked from its original concept, stopped while all four tires were still on the pavement. The cars continue to go fast, and their beauty will endure.

Let's let that thought bring our book to a close.

Performance comes to the kitchen. Carroll Shelby's Original Texas Brand Chili is a national favorite, and older-style packages are considered collectors' items.

Not only did one Shelby owner arrange for a special license tag, but got Carroll Shelby to personalize it.

Index